COLLECTED WORKS OF RENÉ GUÉNON

EAST AND WEST

RENÉ GUÉNON

EAST AND WEST

Translator
Martin Lings

SOPHIA PERENNIS

HILLSDALE NY

Originally published in French as
Orient et Occident
© Les Éditions de la Maisnie 1924
English translation © Sophia Perennis 2001
First English Edition 2001
Second Impression 2004
All rights reserved

Series editor: James R. Wetmore

No part of this book may be reproduced or transmitted,
in any form or by any means, without permission

For information, address:
Sophia Perennis, P.O. Box 611
Hillsdale NY 12529
sophiaperennis.com

Library of Congress Cataloging-in-Publication Data

Guénon, René
[Orient et Occident. English]
East and West / René Guénon ; translated by
Martin Lings

p. cm. — (Collected works of René Guénon)
Includes index.
ISBN 0 900588 34 9 (pbk: alk. paper)
ISBN 0 900588 49 7 (cloth: alk. paper)
1. East and West. 2. Civilization, Western. I. Lings, Martin. II. Title
CB251.G813   2001
909'.09821—dc21   2001000437

CONTENTS

Editorial Note xi
Preface 1

WESTERN ILLUSIONS

1 Civilization and Progress 11
2 The Superstition of Science 27
3 The Superstition of Life 51
4 Imaginary Terrors and Real Dangers 67

HOW THE DIFFERENCES MIGHT BE BRIDGED

1 Fruitless Attempts 85
2 Agreement on Principles 105
3 Constitution of the Elite and the Part to be Played by It 122
4 Not Fusion but Mutual Understanding 139
Conclusion 156
Index 169

EDITORIAL NOTE

THE PAST CENTURY HAS WITNESSED an erosion of earlier cultural values as well as a blurring of the distinctive characteristics of the world's traditional civilizations, giving rise to philosophic and moral relativism, multiculturalism, and dangerous fundamentalist reactions. As early as the 1920s, the French metaphysician René Guénon (1886–1951) had diagnosed these tendencies and presented what he believed to be the only possible reconciliation of the legitimate, although apparently conflicting, demands of outward religious forms, 'exoterisms', with their essential core, 'esoterism'. His works are characterized by a foundational critique of the modern world coupled with a call for intellectual reform; a renewed examination of metaphysics, the traditional sciences, and symbolism, with special reference to the ultimate unanimity of all spiritual traditions; and finally, a call to the work of spiritual realization. Despite their wide influence, translation of Guénon's works into English has so far been piecemeal. The *Sophia Perennis* edition is intended to fill the urgent need to present them in a more authoritative and systematic form. A complete list of Guénon's works, given in the order of their original publication in French, follows this note.

East and West, first published in 1924, was the fourth of a series of books that cleared the ground for Guénon's later writings. His first book, *Introduction to the Study of the Hindu Doctrines* (1921), was an exposition of metaphysics as transmitted in the Hindu tradition, and served to establish his specific use of important terms such as 'esoterism', 'tradition', and 'orthodoxy'. He next set about writing two extensive volumes critiquing what he called 'pseudo-esoteric' groups. The first of these, *Theosophy*: *History of a Pseudo-Religion* (1921), is an exposé of Madame Blavatsky's Theosophical Society; the second, *The Spiritist Fallacy* (1923), examines the current of nineteenth-century spiritism that set the stage for many occult movements that appeared toward the end of that century. Guénon's application of traditional metaphysics to the special case of pseudo-esoteric groups was then broadened in the present book to the general question of East and West as conservators and transmitters of traditional wisdom in the modern age. The titles of its two parts, 'Western Illusions' and 'How the Differences Might be Bridged', describe perfectly the book's intention. Later books, especially *The Crisis of the Modern World* and its magisterial sequel, *The Reign of Quantity and the Signs of the Times*, further extended Guénon's penetrating critique of the modern world.

Guénon often uses words or expressions set off in 'scare quotes'. To avoid clutter, single quotation marks have been used throughout. As for transliterations, Guénon was more concerned with phonetic fidelity than academic usage. The system adopted here reflects the views of scholars familiar both with the languages and Guénon's writings. Brackets indicate editorial insertions, or, within citations, Guénon's additions. Wherever possible, references have been updated, and English editions substituted.

The present translation is based on the work of Martin Lings, published originally under the pseudonym William Massey. Thanks go to John Champoux,, John Ahmed Herlihy, and Benjamin Hardman for editorial reviews, and to Cecil Bethell for proofing and indexing. Cover design by Michael Buchino and Gray Henry, based on a drawing of a 'Sun-door' with rings from the late Bronze Age, by Guénon's friend and collaborator Ananda K. Coomaraswamy.

THE WORKS
OF RENÉ GUÉNON

*Introduction to the Study
of the Hindu Doctrines* (1921)

*Theosophy: History of
a Pseudo-Religion* (1921)

The Spiritist Fallacy (1923)

East and West (1924)

*Man and His Becoming
according to the Vedānta* (1925)

The Esoterism of Dante (1925)

The Crisis of the Modern World
(1927)

The King of the World (1927)

*Spiritual Authority and
Temporal Power* (1929)

The Symbolism of the Cross (1931)

The Multiple States of the Being
(1932)

*The Reign of Quantity and
the Signs of the Times* (1945)

Perspectives on Initiation (1946)

The Great Triad (1946)

*The Metaphysical Principles of
the Infinitesimal Calculus* (1946)

*Initiation and Spiritual
Realization* (1952)

*Insights into Christian
Esoterism* (1954)

Symbols of Sacred Science (1962)

*Studies in Freemasonry
and the Compagnonnage* (1964)

Studies in Hinduism (1966)

*Traditional Forms and Cosmic
Cycles* (1970)

*Insights into Islamic Esoterism
and Taoism* (1973)

Reviews (1973)

Miscellanea (1976)

PREFACE

Rudyard Kipling once wrote these words:

*East is East, and West is West,
And never the twain shall meet.*

It is true, however, that he goes on to modify this statement, admitting that the difference disappears 'when two strong men stand face to face that have come from the ends of the earth'; but even this modification is not really very satisfactory, for it is most unlikely that he had in mind 'strength' of a spiritual order. However that may be, it usually happens that the first verse is quoted by itself, as if all that had stuck in the reader's mind was the idea of the unbridgeable difference which the verse expresses; no doubt this idea represents the opinion held by most Europeans, and it seems to betray in them the dismay of the conqueror who has to admit that those whom he believes he has conquered carry within them something over which he can never have any hold. But whatever feeling may have given rise to such an opinion, what interests us especially is to know whether it is true, or how far it is true; indeed, on considering the present state of things, there are many signs that seem to bear out this opinion; but nonetheless, if we shared it entirely, if we thought that no closer relations are possible, and that none ever will be, we should not have undertaken the writing of this book.

We realize, perhaps more than anyone else, the whole distance that separates East and West, especially the modern West; furthermore, in our *Introduction to the Study of the Hindu Doctrines*, we insisted on the differences so much that some may have thought us inclined to exaggerate. We are, however, convinced that we said nothing that was not rigorously exact, and at the same time we considered in our conclusion whether and how there might be a re-establishment of intellectual relations, which, despite its apparent remoteness, seems to us nonetheless possible. Therefore, if we protested against the attempts of certain Westerners to see likenesses where there are none, it was because illusions of such a nature are not the least obstacle to a proper understanding between East and West; a start based on a false conception often leads in a direction opposite to the one intended. The refusal to see things as they are and to admit certain differences—at present they cannot be too much stressed—involves a complete failure to understand the Eastern mentality, and simply makes the misunderstandings more serious and more permanent, whereas the first efforts should go toward dispelling them. So long as Westerners imagine that there only exists a single type of humanity, that there is only one 'civilization', at different stages of development, no mutual understanding will be possible. The truth is that there are many civilizations, developing along very different lines, and that, among these, that of the modern West is strangely exceptional, as some of its characteristics show. One should never speak absolutely of superiority or inferiority without making it quite clear from what point of view the things to be compared are being considered, even supposing that they are comparable. There is no civilization which is superior to the others from every point of view, because man cannot be equally active at the same time in every direction, and because there are some ways of development which seem actually incompatible with one another. One thing however may be maintained, and this is that there is a certain hierarchy to be observed, and that things of the intellectual order, for example, are worth more than those of the material; if this is so, a civilization which shows itself inferior from the former point of view, in spite of being undeniably superior from the latter, will remain on the whole at a disadvantage, whatever may be the outward appearances; and so it is with Western civilization when compared with those of the East. We are well aware that this way of thinking shocks the great majority of Westerners, because it goes against all their prejudices; but apart from any question of superiority, let them at least admit that the things which in their eyes are of the greatest importance do not necessarily interest all men to the same extent, that some may even consider them utterly negligible, and that there are other ways of showing intelligence than by making machines. It would be at least something if the Europeans came to understand this and behaved accordingly; their relations with the rest of mankind would then be somewhat changed, to the great benefit of the whole world.

But that is only the outermost side of the question: if the people of the West admitted that other civilizations are not necessarily to be altogether despised simply for differing from theirs, there would be nothing further to prevent them from studying these civilizations as they ought to be studied, that is, without the determination to disparage them and without preconceived hostility; and then perhaps a few of them would not be slow to realize, by means of this study, how much they themselves lack, above all from the purely intellectual point of view. Of course, we are supposing that these few would have attained, in some degree at least, the true understanding of the spirit of the different civilizations, and to do this something other is required than efforts of mere scholarship; everyone, no doubt, is not fitted for such an understanding, but if some are, as is after all probable, that alone may lead sooner or later to inestimable results.

We have already alluded to the part that an intellectual elite might play, once it had been formed in the Western world, where it would act as a leaven to move forward, and to direct along the most favorable lines, a mental transformation which, wanted or not, will one day or another become inevitable. Besides, some people are already beginning to feel more or less confusedly that things cannot go on forever as they are now and even speak, as of something possible, of a bankruptcy of Western civilization, which no one would have dared to do a few years ago; but the real causes that may bring about this bankruptcy seem for the most part to escape them still. As these causes are, at the same time, precisely those that prevent any understanding between East and West, there is a double benefit to be had from knowing them: work in preparation for this understanding is at the same time an effort to divert the catastrophes which threaten the West through its own fault; these two ends are much more closely connected than might be supposed. It is not then a task of useless and purely negative criticism to show up, as we intend to do again, the errors and illusions of the West; we are prompted by something far deeper than mere criticism, and we bring with us no intention to 'satirize', which moreover would ill suit our character; if there are some who believe that they have detected anything of the sort in us, they are strangely mistaken. Personally, we would much rather not have to devote ourselves to this task, which is on the whole a thankless one: we would rather be able to rest content in the exposition of certain truths, without ever having to bother ourselves about false interpretations, which, as if out of sheer willfulness, only complicate and confuse matters; but we cannot ignore these contingencies, because, if we do not start by clearing the ground, there is a risk that all we can say will never be understood. Besides, even where we seem to be only clearing away mistakes or replying to objections, we can take the opportunity of bringing to light things that have a really positive significance; and for example, by showing why certain attempts to bring East and West closer have failed, shall we not already be hinting, by contrast, at the conditions in which a similar undertaking might succeed? We hope therefore that our intentions will not be misunderstood, and if we take no pains to cloak the difficulties and obstacles, if on the contrary we insist on them, it is simply that before they can be smoothed away or surmounted, they must be known. We cannot stop at minor considerations and wonder what will be pleasing to some or displeasing to others; the question that we are considering is too serious, even if it be only discussed in what we may call its outward aspects, that is, in what does not concern the order of pure intellect.

Indeed, we do not intend to expound doctrine here, and what we shall say will come, in general, within the scope of more people than did those points of view which we treated in our *Introduction to the Study of the Hindu Doctrines*. But even that was in no way written for a few 'specialists': if some have been deceived in this respect by its title, it is because these questions are as a rule the monopoly of scholars, who study them in a way that might well put others off and that is, in our eyes, devoid of real interest. Our attitude is quite another one: we are essentially concerned, not with scholarship, but with understanding, which is totally different: it is not among the 'specialists' that there is most chance of coming upon the possibilities of a wide and deep understanding, far from it; and, except for some very rare exceptions, it is not they who should be relied on for forming this elite that we have spoken of. Perhaps there are some who are offended that we should attack scholarship, or rather the abuses of it and the dangers it presents, although we have carefully abstained from anything which might seem like a polemic; but one of our motives is precisely that this scholarship, with its peculiar methods, seems to turn away from certain things those very persons who would be most capable of understanding them. Many people seeing the Hindu doctrines mentioned, and thinking at once of the works of one or two orientalists, say to themselves: 'This is not for us'; but some of these are certainly very wrong in thinking so and, perhaps without much effort, they might acquire knowledge, which these very orientalists lack, and always will lack: scholarship is one thing, real knowledge is another, and although not always incompatible, they do not necessarily go together. Assuredly, if scholarship consented to keep to the rank of auxiliary, which it should normally hold, we would have nothing more to reproach it with, since by so doing it would cease to be dangerous and might even be of some use: within these limits, then, we would willingly acknowledge its relative value. There are some cases where the 'historical method' is legitimate, but the mistake which we have protested against consists in believing that it may be applied everywhere, and in wishing to get from it something that it cannot really give. We think we have shown elsewhere,[1] without being in any way inconsistent, that, when necessary, we are just as capable as anyone else of applying this method, and this should be enough to show that we have no prejudice. Each question should be treated according to the method which suits it naturally; it is a singular phenomenon, this confusing of the different orders and different domains with which the West of today never ceases to regale us. In a word, it is necessary to know how to put each thing in its place, and we have never said otherwise: but in so doing one is forced to realize that, despite the manias for

---

1. *Theosophy: History of a Pseudo-Religion.*

equality that possess some of our contemporaries, there are things that can only be secondary and subordinate in comparison with others; and this is why scholarship, even where it is valid, can never be anything but a means, and not an end in itself.

These few explanations seemed to us necessary for several reasons: firstly, we are anxious to say what we think as plainly as possible, and to put an end to any misunderstanding which may arise, as it almost inevitably will, despite our precautions. While admitting in general the clarity of our expositions, people have sometimes attributed to us intentions that we have never had; we shall have here the opportunity of dispelling some uncertainties and of making clear some points about which we may not previously have been explicit enough. Furthermore, the diversity of the subjects that we treat is not opposed to the unity of the conception which presides over them, and we are anxious to affirm expressly this unity, which might escape the notice of those who consider things too superficially. These subjects are indeed so closely connected that, with regard to many of the points we shall touch on here, we should have referred, to make things still clearer, to the complementary information found in our other works; but we have only done so where it seemed absolutely necessary, and for the rest we shall confine ourselves to this general indication, given once and for all, so that the reader may not be wearied by too many references. We should also take this opportunity to say that, where we do not think it suitable to express our thoughts in a strictly doctrinal form, we nonetheless draw constant inspiration from the doctrines whose truth we have understood: it is the study of the Eastern doctrines which has made us see what the West lacks and the falsity of many ideas that are current in the modern world; it is in this study, and there alone, that we have found, as we have already had occasion to state elsewhere, things of which the West has never offered us the slightest equivalent.

We do not in the least pretend to exhaust, in this work any more than in our others, all the questions which may come under consideration: we can hardly be blamed for not putting everything in a single book, which moreover we should be quite unable to do. As for what is merely touched on here, we might take it up again and explain it more fully elsewhere, if circumstances allow; if not, it may at least suggest trains of thought to others, who will benefit enormously in letting them take the place of those developments which we ourselves have been unable to supply. There are some things which are sometimes interesting to note incidentally, even where it is not possible for the moment to treat them at length, and we have often thought it better not to pass them by without at least some reference; but, knowing the mentality of certain people, we feel bound to remark that there is no extraordinary significance to be seen in such a proceeding. We know only too well the import of the so-called 'mysteries' that, in our epoch, have been so much exploited and that are only mysterious because those who speak of them are foremost in understanding nothing about them; there is no true mystery except what is by its very nature inexpressible. We would not however maintain that all truths are always equally ripe for telling, and that there are no cases in which it is not more opportune to keep up a certain reserve and no things which it would be more dangerous than salutary to make public; but this only applies to certain orders of knowledge, on the whole fairly limited, and moreover, if occasionally we come to allude to things of this kind,[2] we do not fail to say so formally, without ever hiding behind any of those chimerical interdictions which the writers of certain schools set up on every occasion, either to provoke their readers' curiosity or simply to cloak their own difficulties. Such tricks are altogether foreign to us, no less so than purely literary fictions; our sole intention is to state the truth, as far as we know it and such as we know it. We cannot say all we think, because that would take us often too far from our subject, and also because thought always goes beyond the limits of the expression in which it is to be enclosed; but we never say anything which we do not really think. That is why we cannot allow our intentions to be falsified and ourselves to be interpreted as saying something other than what we do say, or our words to be turned upside down in search of some entirely imaginary thought hidden

---

2. We have actually come to do so on several occasions in our work *The Spiritist Fallacy*, with regard to certain experimental research, the interest of which does not, we feel, make up for the drawbacks, but the possibility of which we were obliged to indicate through regard for the truth.

beneath them. On the other hand, we shall be always grateful to those who will call our attention to points which they feel should be explained more fully and clearly, and we shall strive to give them subsequent satisfaction; but we beg them to wait until we are able to do so, and not to jump to conclusions from insufficient evidence, and above all we ask them to refrain from holding any doctrine responsible for the imperfections and gaps in our treatise.

WESTERN ILLUSIONS

1

CIVILIZATION AND PROGRESS

The civilization of the modern West appears in history as a veritable anomaly: among all those which are known to us more or less completely, this civilization is the only one that has developed along purely material lines, and this monstrous development, whose beginning coincides with the so-called Renaissance, has been accompanied, as indeed it was fated to be, by a corresponding intellectual regress; we say corresponding and not equivalent, because here are two orders of things between which there can be no common measure. This regress has reached such a point that the Westerners of today no longer know what pure intellect is; in fact they do not even suspect that anything of the kind can exist; hence their disdain, not only for Eastern civilization, but also for the Middle Ages of Europe, whose spirit escapes them scarcely less completely. How is the interest of a purely speculative knowledge to be brought home to people for whom intelligence is nothing but a means of acting on matter and turning it to practical ends, and for whom science, in their limited understanding of it, is above all important insofar as it may be applied to industrial purposes? We exaggerate nothing; it only needs a glance at one's surroundings to realize that this is indeed the mentality of the vast majority of our contemporaries; and another glance, this time at philosophy from Francis Bacon and Descartes onward, could only confirm this impression still further. We will mention, by way of reminder, that Descartes limited intelligence to reason, that he granted to what he thought might be called 'metaphysics' the mere function of serving as a basis for physics, and that this physics itself was by its very nature destined, in his eyes, to pave the way for the applied sciences, mechanical, medicinal, and moral—the final limit of human knowledge as he conceived it. Are not the tendencies which he so affirmed just those that at the first glance may be seen to characterize the whole development of the modern world? To deny or to ignore all pure and supra-rational knowledge was to open up the path which logically could only lead on the one hand to positivism and agnosticism, which resign themselves to the narrowest limitations of intelligence and of its object, and on the other hand to all those sentimental and 'voluntarist' theories that feverishly seek in the infra-rational for what reason cannot give them. Indeed, those of our contemporaries who wish to react against rationalism accept nonetheless the complete identification of intelligence with mere reason, and they believe that it is nothing more than a purely practical faculty, incapable of going beyond the realm of matter. Bergson has written as follows: 'Intelligence, considered in what seems to be its original feature, is the faculty of manufacturing artificial objects, in particular tools to make tools [sic], and of indefinitely varying the manufacture.'[1] And again: 'Intelligence, even when it no longer operates upon its own object (i.e., brute matter), follows habits it has contracted in that operation: it applies forms that are indeed those of unorganized matter. It is made for this kind of work. With this kind of work alone is it fully satisfied. And that is what intelligence expresses by saying that thus only it arrives at distinctness and clearness.'[2] From these last features it becomes obvious that there is no question here of intelligence itself, but quite simply of the Cartesian conception of intelligence, which is very different: and the 'new philosophy', as its adherents call it, substitutes for the superstition of reason another that is in some respects still grosser, namely, the superstition of life. Rationalism, though powerless to attain to absolute truth, at least allowed relative truth to subsist; the intuitionism of today lowers that truth to be nothing more than a representation of sensible reality, in all its inconsistency and ceaseless change; finally, pragmatism succeeds in blotting out altogether the very notion of truth by identifying it with

---

1. *Creative Evolution*, p146, in the English translation of Arthur Mitchell.
2. Ibid., p169.

that of utility, which amounts to suppressing it purely and simply. We may have schematized things a little here, but we have not falsified them in the least, and whatever may have been the intermediate stages, the fundamental tendencies are indeed those we have just stated; the pragmatists, in going to the limit, show themselves to be the most authentic representatives of modern Western thought: what does the truth matter in a world whose aspirations, being solely material and sentimental and not intellectual, find complete satisfaction in industry and morality, two spheres where indeed one can very well do without conceiving the truth? To be sure, this extremity was not reached at a single stride, and many Europeans will protest that they have not reached it yet; but we are thinking particularly of the Americans, who are at a more 'advanced' stage of the same civilization. Mentally as well as geographically, modern America is indeed the 'Far West'; and Europe will follow, without any doubt, if nothing comes to stop the development of the consequences implied in the present state of things.

But most extraordinary of all is perhaps the claim to set up this abnormal civilization as the very type of all civilization, to regard it as 'the civilization' par excellence, and even as the only one that deserves the name. Extraordinary too, and also complementary to this illusion is the belief in 'progress', considered no less absolutely, and naturally identified, at heart, with this material development that absorbs the entire activity of the modern West. It is curious to note how promptly and successfully certain ideas come to spread and impose themselves, provided of course that they correspond to the general tendencies of the particular environment and epoch; it is so with these ideas of 'civilization' and 'progress', which so many people willingly believe universal and necessary, whereas in reality they have been quite recently invented and, even today, at least three-quarters of mankind persist either in being ignorant of them or in considering them quite negligible. Jacques Bainville has remarked that:

> If the verb *civilize* is already found to have been used by the good authors of the eighteenth century in the sense which we give it, the noun *civilization* is only to be met with in the economists of

the years which immediately preceded the French Revolution. Littré quotes an example taken from Turgot. Littré, who had ransacked all French literature, could not trace it any further back. Thus the word civilization has no more than a century and a half of existence. It was only in 1835, less than a hundred years ago, that it finally found its way into the dictionary of the Academy.... The ancients, from whom we still consciously trace our descent, were equally without a term for what we mean by civilization. If this word were given to be translated in Latin prose, the schoolboy would indeed find himself in difficulties.... The life of words is not independent of the life of ideas. The word civilization, which our ancestors did very well without, perhaps because they had the thing itself, spread during the nineteenth century under the influence of new ideas. The scientific discoveries, the development of industry, of commerce, of prosperity and of material welfare, had created a kind of enthusiasm and even a kind of 'prophetics'. The conception of indefinite progress, dating from the second half of the eighteenth century, helped to convince mankind that it had entered upon a new era, that of absolute civilization. It is the now quite forgotten Fourier, an utter utopian, who was responsible for first calling the present age the age of civilization, and for identifying civilization with modern times.... So civilization was the degree of development and perfection which the nations of Europe had reached in the nineteenth century. This term, understood by everyone, although no one had defined it, included material and moral progress side by side, the one bringing with it the other, the one united to the other, both inseparable. In a word, civilization was Europe itself, it was a patent which the European world granted itself.[3]

That is exactly what we think ourselves; and we were intent on making this quotation, although it is rather long, to show that we are not alone in thinking so.

3. 'L' Avenir de la Civilization', *Revue Universelle*, March 1, 1922, pp 586–587.

CIVILIZATION AND PROGRESS   15

These two ideas, then, of 'civilization' and 'progress', which are very closely connected, both date only from the second half of the eighteenth century, that is to say from the epoch which saw, among other things, the birth of materialism;[4] and they were propagated and popularized especially by the socialist dreamers of the beginning of the nineteenth century. It cannot be denied that the history of ideas leads sometimes to rather surprising observations, and helps to reduce certain fantastic ideas to their proper value; it would do so more than ever if it were not, as is moreover the case with ordinary history, falsified by biased interpretations, or limited to efforts of mere scholarship and to pointless research into questions of detail. True history might endanger certain political interests; and it may be wondered if this is not the reason, where education is concerned, why certain methods are officially imposed to the exclusion of all others: consciously or not, they begin by removing everything that might make it possible to see certain things clearly, and that is how 'public opinion' is formed. But to go back to the two ideas that we have just been speaking of, let us make it quite clear that in giving them so close an origin we have in mind simply this absolute and, as we think, illusory interpretation, which is the one most usually given them today. As for the relative meaning in which the same words may be used, that is quite another question, and as this meaning is very legitimate, there can be no question here of ideas that originated at some definite moment; it matters little that they may have been expressed in one way or another and, if a term is convenient, it is not because of its recent creation that we see disadvantages in using it. Thus we do not hesitate to say that there have been and still are many different 'civilizations'; it would be rather hard to define exactly this complex assemblage of elements of different orders which make up what is called a civilization, but even so

---

4. The word 'materialism' was invented by Berkeley, who only used it to designate belief in the reality of matter; materialism in its modern sense, that is to say the theory that nothing exists but matter, originates only with La Mettrie and Holbach; it should not be confused with mechanism, several examples of which are to be found even among the ancients.

everyone knows fairly well what is to be understood by it. We do not even think it necessary to try to enclose in a rigid formula either the general characteristics of civilization as a whole, or the special characteristics of some particular civilization; that is a somewhat artificial process, and we greatly distrust these narrow 'pigeon-holes' that the systematic turn of mind delights in. Just as there are 'civilizations', there are also, during the development of each of them, or for certain more or less limited periods of this development, 'progresses' which, far from influencing everything indiscriminately, affect only this or that particular domain; in fact this is only another way of saying that a civilization develops along certain lines and in a certain direction; but just as there are progresses, there are also regresses, and sometimes the two are brought about at one and the same time in different domains. We insist, then, that all this is eminently relative; if the same words are accepted in an absolute sense they no longer correspond to any reality, and it is then that they come to represent these new ideas which have existed for barely a century and a half, and then only in the West. Certainly 'Progress' and 'Civilization', with capital letters, may be very effective in certain sentences, as hollow as they are rhetorical, most suitable for imposing on a mob, for which words are rather a substitute for thought than a means of expressing it, thus it is that these two words play one of the most important parts in the battery of formulas which those 'in control' today use to accomplish their strange task of collective suggestion without which the mentality that is characteristic of modern times would indeed be short-lived. In this respect we doubt whether enough notice has ever been given to the analogy, which is nonetheless striking, between, for example, the actions of the orator and the hypnotist (and that of the animal-tamer belongs equally to the same class); here is another subject for the psychologists to study, and we call their attention to it in passing. No doubt the power of words has been more or less made use of in other times than ours; but what has no parallel is this gigantic collective hallucination by which a whole section of humanity has come to take the vainest fantasies for incontestable realities; and, among these idols of modern worship, the two which we are at the moment denouncing are perhaps the most pernicious of all.

We must revert again to the birth of the idea of progress, or rather of indefinite progress, to exclude these particular and limited progresses whose existence we have not the least desire to dispute. It is probably in the writings of Pascal that the first trace of this idea is to be found, applied moreover to a single point of view: the passage[5] is the well-known one where he compares humanity to 'one and the same man who always exists and who learns continually during the course of the centuries,' and where he shows evidence of that anti-traditional spirit that is one of the peculiarities of the modern West, declaring that 'those whom we call ancient were actually new in everything,' and that consequently their opinions have very little weight; and in this respect Pascal had at least one predecessor, since Bacon had already said with the same implication: *Antiquitas saeculi, juventus mundi*. The unconscious sophism that such a conception is based on is easy to see: it consists in supposing that humanity as a whole develops continuously along the same lines: the false simplicity in this outlook is quite blatant, since it is in contradiction with all the known facts. Indeed, history shows us, at every epoch, civilizations independent of one another, often divergent, some of which are born and develop while others grow decadent and die, or are annihilated at one blow in some cataclysm; and the new civilizations by no means always gather in the inheritance of the old ones. Who would venture to maintain seriously, for example, that the West of today has benefited, however indirectly, by the knowledge which the Chaldeans or the Egyptians had accumulated, let alone some civilizations that have not even come down to us in name? But there is no need to go back so far into the past, as there are sciences that were studied in Europe during the Middle Ages, and of which there remains no longer the least notion. If Pascal's idea of 'collective' man (whom he very improperly calls 'universal man') is to be kept, it must then be said that, if there are periods in which he learns, there are others in which he forgets, or rather, that while he learns certain things he forgets others; but the reality is even more complex, since there are simultaneously, as there have always been, civilizations which do not penetrate one another, but remain

---

5. Fragment of *Traité du Vide*.

unknown to each other: that is indeed, today more than ever, the situation of the Western civilization with regard to the Eastern ones. All told, the origin of the illusion expressed by Pascal is simply this: the people of the West, starting from the Renaissance, took to considering themselves exclusively as the heirs and carriers-on of Greco-Roman antiquity, and to misunderstanding or ignoring all the rest; that is what we call the 'classical prejudice'. The humanity that Pascal speaks of begins with the Greeks, continues with the Romans, and then there is a discontinuity in its existence corresponding to the Middle Ages, in which he can only see, like all the people of the seventeenth century, a period of sleep; then at last comes the Renaissance, that is, the awakening of this humanity, which, from then on, is to be composed of all the European peoples together. It is a grotesque error, and one that indicates a strangely limited mental horizon, consisting, as it does, in taking the part for the whole. Its influence may be found in more than one sphere: the psychologists, for example, usually confine their observations to a single type of humanity, the modern Westerner, and stretch inadmissibly the results so obtained even to the pretension of drawing from them, without exception, the characteristics of man in general.

It is essential to remember that Pascal only visualized an intellectual progress, within the limits of his and his time's conception of intellectuality; it was toward the very end of the eighteenth century that there appeared, with Turgot and Condorcet, the idea of progress extended to all branches of activity; and this idea was then so far from being generally accepted that Voltaire eagerly set about ridiculing it. We cannot think of giving here the complete history of the different modifications which this same idea underwent during the nineteenth century, and of the pseudo-scientific complications in which it was involved when, under the name of 'evolution', people sought to apply it, not only to humanity, but to the whole animal world. Evolutionism, despite many more or less important divergencies, has become a real official dogma: it is taught like a law which it is forbidden to discuss, when actually it is nothing more than the most idle and ill-founded of all hypotheses; this applies *a fortiori* to the conception of human progress, which is now taken for granted as being no more than a particular case of 'evolution'. But before reaching this position there were many ups and downs, and, even among the champions of progress, there were some who could not help making one or two rather serious reservations: Auguste Comte, who had started by being a disciple of Saint-Simon, admitted a progress that was indefinite in duration but not in extent; for him the march of humanity might be represented by a curve with an asymptote which it approaches indefinitely without ever reaching, so that the extent of progress possible, that is to say the distance from the present state to the ideal state, represented by the distance from the curve to the asymptote, grows perpetually less. Nothing is easier than to show the confusions that underlie the fantastic theory which Comte named the 'law of the three states', and of which the chief consists in supposing that the sole object of all possible knowledge is the explanation of natural phenomena. Like Bacon and Pascal he compared the ancients to children, and others, more recently, have thought to improve on this by likening them to the savages, whom they call 'primitives', but whom we on the contrary consider degenerates.[6] Apart from these there are some who, unable to help noticing the ups and downs in what they know of the history of mankind, have come to talk of a 'rhythm of progress'; it would be perhaps simpler and more logical in these circumstances to stop talking about progress altogether, but, since the modern dogma must be safe-guarded at all costs, progress is supposed to exist nonetheless as the final result of all the partial progresses and all the regresses. These reservations and disagreements ought to serve as food for reflection, but very few seem to have realized this. The different schools can come to no mutual agreement, but it remains understood that progress and evolution must be admitted; without these it seems that one would lose all right to the title of 'civilized man'.

6. Despite the influence of the 'sociological school', there are, even in 'official circles', some authorities who agree with us on this point, notably Georges Foucart, who, in the introduction of his work entitled *Histoire des religions et Methode comparative*, upholds the theory of 'degeneration', and mentions several of its supporters. In connection with this, Foucart criticizes admirably the 'sociological school' and its methods, and he very properly declares that 'totemism or sociology should not be confused with serious ethnology.'

There is still another point that is worth noticing: if one examines which branches of the pretended progress most often come up for consideration today, which ones are imagined by our contemporaries to be the starting-point of all the rest, it will be seen that they only amount to two: 'material progress' and 'moral progress'. These are the only ones mentioned by Jacques Bainville as included in the current idea of 'civilization', and we think he was right. To be sure, there are some who still talk about 'intellectual progress', but for them this phrase is essentially a synonym of 'scientific progress', and it applies above all to the development of the experimental sciences and of their applications. Here again there comes to light this degradation of intelligence which ends in identifying it with the most limited and inferior of all its uses—experimenting upon matter for solely practical purposes. To be accurate, the so-called 'intellectual progress' is thus no more than 'material progress' itself, and, if intelligence was only that, Bergson's definition of it would have to be accepted. Actually it never enters the heads of most Westerners of today that intelligence is anything else; for them it no longer amounts even to reason in its Cartesian sense, but to the lowest part of this reason, to its most elementary functions, to what always remains closely connected with this world of the senses which they have made the one exclusive field of their activity. For those who know that there is something else and who persist in giving words their true meaning, there can be no question in our time of 'intellectual progress', but on the contrary of decadence, or to be still more accurate, of intellectual ruin; and, because there are some lines of development which are incompatible, it is precisely this which is the forfeit paid for 'material progress', the only progress whose existence during the last centuries is a real fact: it may be called scientific progress if one insists, but only in an extremely limited meaning of the word, and a progress that is very much more industrial than scientific. Material development and pure intellectuality go in opposite directions; he who sinks himself in the one becomes necessarily further removed from the other. It should be carefully noted that we say here intellectuality and not rationality, for the domain of reason is only intermediate, as it were, between that of the senses and that of the higher intellect: though reason receives a reflection of intellect, even while denying it and believing itself to be the human being's highest faculty, it is always from the evidence of the senses that the notions which it works on are drawn. In other words, what is general, the proper object of reason and consequently of the science which is reason's work, though it is not of the sensible order of things, proceeds nonetheless from what is individual, which is perceived by the senses; it may be said to be beyond the sensible, but not above it; it is only the universal, the object of pure intellect, that is transcendent, and in the light of the universal even the general itself becomes one with the individual. That is the fundamental distinction between metaphysical knowledge and scientific knowledge, such as we have shown it to be more fully elsewhere;[7] and, if we call attention to it again here, it is because the total absence of the former and the disordered development of the latter are the most striking characteristics of the Western civilization in its present state.

As for the conception of 'moral progress', it represents the other predominant factor in the modern mentality, that is, sentimentality. The presence of this element does not serve in the least to make us modify the judgment which we formulated in saying that the Western civilization is altogether material. We are well aware that some people seek to oppose the domain of sentiment to that of matter, to make the development of the one a sort of counterbalance against the spread of the other, and to take for their ideal an equilibrium as settled as possible between these two complementary elements. Such is perhaps, when all is said and done, the thought of the intuitionists who, associating intelligence inseparably with matter, hope to deliver themselves from it with the help of a rather vaguely defined instinct. Such is still more certainly the thought of the pragmatists, who make utility a substitute for truth and consider it at one and the same time under its material and moral aspects; and we see here too how fully pragmatism expresses the particular tendencies of the modern world, and above all of the Anglo-Saxon world, which is one of its most typical portions. Indeed, materialism and sentimentality, far from being in opposition, can scarcely exist one

---

7. *Introduction to the Study of the Hindu Doctrines*, pt 2, chap. 5.

without the other, and they both attain side by side to their maximum development; the proof of this lies in America, where, as we have had occasion to remark in our books on Theosophism and Spiritualism, the worst pseudo-mystical extravagances come to birth and spread with incredible ease at the very time when industrialism and the passion for 'business' are being carried to a pitch that borders on madness; when things have reached this state it is no longer an equilibrium which is set up between the two tendencies, but two disequilibriums side by side which aggravate each other, instead of counterbalancing. It is easy to see the cause of this phenomenon: where intellectuality is reduced to a minimum, it is quite natural that sentiment should assume the mastery; and sentiment, in itself, is very close to the material order of things: there is nothing, in all that concerns psychology, more narrowly dependent on organism, and, in spite of Bergson, it is obviously sentiment and not intellect that is bound up with matter. The intuitionists may reply, as we are well aware, that intelligence, such as they conceive it, is bound up with inorganic matter (it is always Cartesian mechanics and its derivations that they have in mind) and sentiment with living matter, which seems to them to rank higher in the scale of existences. But whether inorganic or living, it is always matter, and in its domain there can never be any but sensible things; it is indeed impossible for the modern mentality, and for the philosophers who represent it, to escape from this limitation. Strictly speaking, if it be insisted that there are two different tendencies here, then one must be assigned to matter and one to life, and this distinction may serve as a fairly satisfactory way of classing the great superstitions of our epoch; but we repeat, they both belong to the same order of things and cannot really be dissociated from each other; they are on one same plane, and not superposed in hierarchy. It follows then that the 'moralism'[8] of our contemporaries is really nothing but the necessary complement of their practical materialism; and it would be an utter illusion to seek to exalt one to the detriment of the other

---

8. We say practical materialism to denote a tendency and to distinguish it from philosophic materialism, which is a theory, and on which this tendency is not necessarily dependent.

because, going necessarily together, they both develop simultaneously along the same lines, which are those of what is termed, by common accord, 'civilization'.

We have just seen why the conceptions of 'material progress' and 'moral progress' are inseparable, and why our contemporaries are almost as indefatigably engrossed with the latter as they are with the former. We have in no way contested the existence of 'material progress', but only its importance: we maintain that it is not worth the intellectual loss which it causes, and it is impossible to think differently without being altogether ignorant of true intellectuality. Now, what is to be thought of the reality of 'moral progress'? That is a question which it is scarcely possible to discuss seriously, because, in this realm of sentiment, everything depends on individual appreciation and preferences; everyone gives the name 'progress' to what is in conformity with his own inclinations, and, in a word, it is impossible to say that one is right any more than another. Those whose tendencies are in harmony with those of their time cannot be other than satisfied with the present state of things, and this is what they express after their fashion when they say that this epoch marks a progress over those that preceded it; but often this satisfaction of their sentimental aspirations is only relative, because the sequence of events is not always what they would have wished, and that is why they suppose that the progress will be continued during future epochs. The facts come sometimes to belie those who are convinced of the present reality of 'moral progress', according to the most usual conception of it; but all they do is modify their ideas a little in this respect, or refer the realization of their ideal to a more or less remote future, and they, too, might crawl out of their difficulties by talking about a 'rhythm of progress'. Besides this, by a much simpler solution, they usually strive to forget the lesson of experience: such are the incorrigible dreamers who, at each new war, do not fail to prophesy that it will be the last. The belief in indefinite progress is, all told, nothing more than the most ingenuous and the grossest of all kinds of 'optimism'; whatever forms this belief may take, it is always sentimental in essence, even when it is concerned with 'material progress'. If it be objected that we ourselves have recognized the existence of this progress, we reply that we have only done so as far as the facts warrant, which does not in the least imply an admission that it should, or even that it can, continue its course indefinitely; furthermore, as we are far from thinking it the best thing in the world, instead of calling it progress we would rather call it quite simply development; it is not in itself that the word progress offends us, but because of the idea of 'value' that has come almost invariably to be attached to it. This brings us to another point: there is indeed also a reality which cloaks itself under the so-called 'moral progress', or which, in other words, keeps up the illusion of it; this reality is the development of sentimentalism, which, whether one likes it or not, does actually exist in the modern world, just as incontestably as does the development of industry and commerce (and we have said why one does not go without the other). This development, in our eyes excessive and abnormal, cannot fail to seem a progress to those who put feelings above everything; and it may perhaps be said that in speaking of mere preferences, as we did not long ago, we have robbed ourselves in advance of the right to confute them. But we have done nothing of the kind: what we said then applies to sentiment, and to sentiment taken alone, in its variations from one individual to another: if sentiment, considered in general, is to be put into its proper place in relation to intelligence, the case is quite different, because then there is a hierarchy to be observed. The modern world has precisely reversed the natural relations between the different orders of things: once again, it is depreciation of the intellectual order (and even absence of pure intellectuality), and exaggeration of the material and the sentimental orders, which all go together to make the Western civilization of today an anomaly, not to say a monstrosity.

That is how things look when considered without any prejudice; and that is how they are seen by the most qualified representatives of the Eastern civilizations who view them quite without bias, for bias is always something sentimental, not intellectual, and their point of view is purely intellectual. If the people of the West have some difficulty in understanding this attitude, it is because they are incorrigibly prone to judge others according to themselves, and to attribute to them their own concerns, as well as their own ways of thinking, and their mental horizon is so narrow that they do not even take into account the possibility of other ones existing; hence their utter failure to understand all the Eastern conceptions. This failure is not reciprocated: the Easterners, when they are faced with Western science, and when they are willing to give themselves the trouble, have scarcely any difficulty in penetrating and understanding its special branches, because they are used to far wider and deeper speculations, and he who can do the greater can do the less; but in general they feel scarcely any temptation to devote themselves to this work, which, for the sake of things that in their eyes are insignificant, might make them lose sight of, or at least neglect, what is for them the essential. Western science means analysis and dispersion; Eastern knowledge means synthesis and concentration; but we shall have occasion to come back to this point. In any case, what the Westerners call civilization, the others would call barbarity, because it is precisely lacking in the essential, that is to say a principle of a higher order. By what right do Westerners claim to impose on everyone their own likes and dislikes? Besides, they should not forget that among earthly mankind taken as a whole they form only a minority; of course, this consideration of number proves nothing in our eyes, but it ought to make some impression on people who have invented 'universal suffrage', and who believe in its efficacy. If they merely took pleasure in affirming their imagined superiority, the illusion would only do harm to themselves; but their most terrible offence is their proselytizing fury: in them the spirit of conquest goes under the disguise of 'moralist' pretexts, and it is in the name of 'liberty' that they would force the whole world to imitate them! Most astonishing of all, they genuinely imagine in their infatuation that they enjoy prestige among all other peoples; because they are dreaded as a brutal force is dreaded, they believe themselves to be admired; when a man is in danger of being crushed by an avalanche, does it follow that he is smitten with respect and admiration for it? The only impression that, for example, mechanical inventions make on most Easterners is one of deep repulsion; certainly it all seems to them far more harmful than beneficial, and if they find themselves obliged to accept certain things which the present epoch has made necessary, they do so in the hope of future riddance; these things do not interest them, and they will never really interest them. What Westerners call progress is for nothing but change and instability; and the need for change, so characteristic of modern times, is in their eyes a mark of manifest inferiority: he who has reached a state of equilibrium no longer feels this need, just as he who has found no longer seeks. In these circumstances it is indeed difficult to understand one another, since the same facts give rise, on this side and on that, to interpretations that are diametrically opposed. What if the Easterners also sought, after the manner of the West, and by its methods, to impose their own outlook? But one may rest assured that nothing is more contrary to their nature than propaganda, and that such considerations are quite foreign to them. Without preaching 'liberty', they let others think what they will, and are even indifferent as to what is thought of them. All they ask, in fact, is to be left in peace, but that is just what the people of the West refuse to allow them, and it must be remembered that they went to seek them out in their own home, and have behaved there in a way that might well exasperate the most peaceful of men. We are thus faced with a state of affairs that cannot last indefinitely; there is only one way for the West to make itself bearable: this is, to use the customary language of colonial politics, that it should give up 'assimilation' and practice instead 'association' in every domain; but that alone would already mean some modification of their mentality, and the understanding of at least one or two of the ideas which form part of our present exposition.

2

THE SUPERSTITION
OF SCIENCE

The civilization of the modern West has, among other pretensions, that of being eminently 'scientific'; it would be as well to make it a little clearer how this term is to be understood, but that is not what is usually done, for it is one of those words to which our contemporaries seem to attach a sort of mysterious power, independent of their meaning. 'Science', with a capital letter, like 'Progress' and 'Civilization', like 'Right', 'Justice', and 'Liberty', is another of those entities that are better left undefined, and that run the risk of losing all their prestige as soon as they are inspected a little too closely. In this way all the so-called 'conquests' which the modern world is so proud of amount to high-sounding words behind which there is nothing, or else something insignificant: we have called it collective suggestion, and the illusion which it leads to, kept up as it is and shared by so many people, cannot possibly be spontaneous. Perhaps one day we will try to throw a little light on this side of the question. But for the moment that is not what we are directly concerned with. We simply note that the modern West believes in the ideas which we have just mentioned, if indeed they may be called ideas, however this belief may have come to it. They are not really ideas, because many of those who pronounce these words with the greatest conviction have in mind nothing very clear that corresponds to them; actually there is nothing there in most cases but the expression—one might even say the personification—of more or less vague sentimental aspirations. These are veritable idols, the divinities of a sort of 'lay religion', which is not clearly defined, no doubt, and which cannot be, but which has nonetheless a very real existence: it is not religion in the proper sense of the word, but it is what pretends to take its place, and what better deserves to be called 'counter-religion'. The origin of this state of things can be traced back to the very beginning of the modern epoch, where the anti-traditional spirit showed itself at once by the proclaiming of 'free inquiry', or in other words, the absence in the doctrinal order of any principle higher than individual opinions. The inevitable result was intellectual anarchy; hence the indefinite multiplicity of religious and pseudo-religious sects, philosophic systems aiming above all at originality, and scientific theories as pretentious as they are ephemeral, in short, unbelievable chaos which is, however, dominated by a certain unity, there being beyond doubt a specifically modern outlook which is the source of it all, though this unity is altogether negative since it is nothing more or less than an absence of principle, expressed by that indifference with regard to truth and error which ever since the eighteenth century has been called 'tolerance'. Let our meaning be quite clear: we have no intention of blaming practical tolerance as applied to individuals, but only theoretic tolerance, which claims to be applied to ideas as well and to recognize the same rights for them all, which if taken logically can only imply a rooted skepticism. Moreover we cannot help noticing that, like all propagandists, the apostles of tolerance, truth to tell, are very often the most intolerant of men. This is what has in fact happened, and it is strangely ironical: those who wished to overthrow all dogma have created for their own use, we will not say a new dogma, but a caricature of dogma, which they have succeeded in imposing on the Western world in general; in this way there have been established, under the pretext of 'freedom of thought', the most chimerical beliefs that have ever been seen at any time, under the form of these different idols, of which we have just singled out some of the more important.

Of all the superstitions preached by those very people who profess that they never stop inveighing against 'superstition', that of 'science' and 'reason' is the only one which does not seem, at first sight, to be based on sentiment; but there is a kind of rationalism that is nothing more than sentimentalism disguised, as is shown only too well by the passion with which its champions uphold it, and by the hatred they evince for whatever goes against their inclinations or passes their comprehension. Besides, since rationalism in any case corresponds to a lessening of intellectuality, it is natural that its development should go hand in hand with that of sentimentalism, as we explained in the last chapter; but either one of these two tendencies may be more particularly represented by certain individualities or by certain currents of thought, and, by reason of the more or less exclusive and systematic terms in which they have come to be clothed, there may even be apparent conflicts between them, which hide their fundamental fellowship from the eyes of superficial onlookers. Modern rationalism begins, in short, with Descartes (it had even had some forerunners in the sixteenth century) and its tracks can be followed throughout all modern philosophy, no less than in the domain which is properly speaking scientific. The present reaction of intuitionism and pragmatism against this rationalism gives us an example of one of these conflicts, and we have seen meanwhile that Bergson entirely accepts the Cartesian definition of intelligence; it is not the nature of intelligence that is questioned, but only its supremacy. In the eighteenth century there was also antagonism between the rationalism of the encyclopedists and the sentimentalism of Rousseau; both these, however, served equally to further the revolutionary movement, which shows that each of them has its place in the negative unity of the anti-traditional outlook. If we cite this example in connection with the preceding one, it is not that we attribute any hidden political motive to Bergson; but we cannot help thinking of the use made of his ideas in certain syndicalist circles, especially in England, while in other circles of the same kind the 'scientific' spirit is held more in honor than ever. Indeed, one of the great tricks of those who 'control' the modern mentality seems to consist, as it were, in brewing a potion for the public, now of rationalism, now of sentimentalism, and now of both together, as occasion demands, and their knack for holding a balance between the two shows that they are much more concerned with their own political interests than with the intellectuality of their patient. It is true that this cleverness may not always be calculated, and we have no desire to question the sincerity of any scientist, historian, or philosopher; but they are often only the apparent 'controllers', and they may be themselves controlled or influenced without in the least realizing it. Besides, the use made of their ideas does not always correspond with their own intentions, and it would be wrong to make them directly responsible, or to blame them for not having foreseen certain more or less remote consequences. But provided that these ideas conform to one or the other of these two tendencies, they may be used in the way which we have just described; and, given the state of intellectual anarchy in which the West is plunged, each event would seem to suggest that every possible advantage is being taken of the disorder itself and of all that contributes to the chaotic agitation for the realizing of a rigidly determined plan. We do not want to insist on this too much, but we find it difficult not to revert to it from time to time, for we cannot admit that a whole race may be purely and simply smitten with a sort of madness which has lasted for several centuries, and there must be something after all which gives a meaning to modern civilization: we do not believe in chance, and we are sure that every existing thing must have a cause; those who think differently are at liberty to set aside such considerations.

Now, taking the two chief tendencies of the modern mentality in turn to examine them better, and leaving for the moment sentimentalism to return to it later, we may ask ourselves this question: what exactly is this 'science' that the West is so infatuated with? A Hindu, summing up most concisely the opinion of all the Easterners who have come across it, has said most justly: 'Western science is ignorant knowledge.'[1] This expression is in no way a contradiction in terms and this is what it means: it is, if one insists, a knowledge that has some reality, since it is valid and effective in one relative domain; but it is a hopelessly limited knowledge, ignorant of the essential, a knowledge which, like everything else that belongs in particular to Western civilization, lacks a principle. Science, as conceived by our contemporaries, is nothing more than the study of sensible phenomena, and this study is undertaken and followed out

1. 'The Miscarriage of Life in the West', by P. Ramanathan, Solicitor-General of Ceylon: *Hibbert Journal*, VII, 1; quoted by Benjamin Kidd, *The Science of Power*, p95.

in such a way that it cannot, we insist, be attached to any principle of a higher order; it is true that by resolutely ignoring everything that lies beyond its scope, it makes itself fully independent in its own domain, but this vaunted independence is only made possible by the limitations of science itself. Not content with that, it goes even to the length of denying what it is ignorant of, because only in this way can it avoid admitting this ignorance: or, if it does not venture in so many words to deny the possible existence of what does not come within its range, it at least denies all possibility of knowing such things, which amounts to the same thing, and it has the pretension of comprising in itself everything that can be known. Starting often unconsciously from a false assumption, the 'scientists' imagine, as did Auguste Comte, that man has never aimed at knowing anything other than an explanation of natural phenomena; we say unconsciously, because they are evidently incapable of understanding that it is possible to go further, and it is not for this that we blame them, but only for their pretension of refusing to allow others the possession or the use of faculties which they themselves lack. They are like blind men who deny, if not light itself, at least the existence of sight, for the sole reason that they are without it. To declare that there is not only an unknown but also an 'unknowable' (to use Spencer's word), and to turn an intellectual infirmity into a barrier which no one may pass—that is something whose like was never seen or heard before; and it is equally unheard of for men to turn a declaration of ignorance into a program of thought and a profession of faith, and quite openly to label a so-called doctrine with it under the name of 'agnosticism'. And these men, be it noted, are not skeptics, and do not wish to be skeptics: if they were, there would be a certain logic in their attitude, which might make it excusable; but they are, on the contrary, the most enthusiastic believers in 'science', the most fervent admirers of 'reason'. It might well be considered rather strange to put reason above everything, to profess a veritable worship for it, and to proclaim at the same time that it is essentially limited; that is, in fact, somewhat contradictory, and though we note it, we do not undertake to explain it; this attitude points to a mentality which is not in the least our own, and it is not for us to justify the contradictions that seem inherent in 'relativism' in all its forms. We, too, say that reason is limited and relative: but, far from making it the whole of intelligence, we look on it only as one of its inferior parts, and we see in intelligence other possibilities that go far beyond those of reason. It seems then that modern Europeans, or at least some of them, are very willing to acknowledge their ignorance, and the rationalists of today do so perhaps more readily than their predecessors, but it is only on condition that no one has the right to know what they themselves do not; the pretension of limiting what is, or just of limiting knowledge fundamentally, shows in either case the spirit of negation which is so characteristic of the modern world. This spirit of negation is nothing other than the systematic spirit, for a system is essentially a closed conception; and it has come to be identified with the spirit of philosophy itself, especially since Kant, who, wishing to shut up all knowledge within the bounds of relativity, ventured to declare in so many words that 'philosophy is not a means of extending knowledge but a discipline for limiting it,'[2] which amounts to saying that the chief function of philosophers is to impose on all the narrow limits of their own understanding. That is why modern philosophy ends by almost entirely substituting 'criticism' or the 'theory of knowledge' for knowledge itself; that is also why many of its representatives no longer claim for it a higher title than 'scientific philosophy', or, in other words, mere coordination of the most general results of science, whose domain is the only one it recognizes as being accessible to intelligence. In these circumstances philosophy and science are not to be distinguished, and in actual fact, since the birth of rationalism, they can only have had one and the same object, they have only represented a single order of knowledge, they have been animated by the self-same spirit: it is this that we call, not the scientific spirit, but the 'scientistic' spirit.

We must insist a little on this last distinction: what we wish to indicate by it is that we see no essential harm in the development of certain sciences, even if we find that far too much importance is given them; it is only a very relative knowledge, but it is nonetheless a knowledge, and it is right that everyone should turn his intellectual activity to what suits his natural talents and the means at his

---

2. Kant, *Kritik der reinen Vernunft*, ed. Hartenstein, p256.

disposal. What we object to is the exclusiveness, we might say the sectarianism, of those who are so intoxicated by the lengths to which these sciences have been stretched that they refuse to admit the existence of anything apart from them, and maintain that, to be valid, every speculation must be submitted to the methods that are peculiar to these same sciences, as if these methods, created for the study of certain fixed objects, were universally applicable. It is true that their conception of universality is something very limited, which certainly does not pass beyond the domain of contingency, but these 'scientists' would be most astonished if told that, without even leaving this domain, there is a host of things which cannot be attained by their methods and which notwithstanding may be made the object of sciences quite different from the ones they know, but no less real and often more interesting in many respects. It seems that people today have arbitrarily accepted, in the domain of scientific knowledge, a certain number of fields, which they have frenziedly set about studying to the exclusion of all the rest and on the assumption that the rest is non-existent; and it is quite natural, and not in the least surprising or admirable, that they should have given these particular sciences which they have so cultivated a much larger development than could men who did not attach anything like the same importance to them, who often scarcely even bothered about them, and who were in any case concerned with many other things which seemed to them more important. We are thinking above all of the considerable development of the experimental sciences, a domain where the modern West clearly excels and where no one would dream of contesting its superiority which, moreover, as the Easterners see it, is a scarcely enviable one for the very reason that it could only be purchased at the expense of forgetting all that they hold truly worthy of interest. However, we have no hesitation in stating that there are sciences, even experimental ones, of which the modern West has not the least idea. Such sciences exist in the East, among those which we call 'traditional sciences'. Even in the West there were also, during the Middle Ages, such sciences, altogether equivalent in some respects; and these sciences, some of which even give rise to undeniably efficient practical applications, are carried out by means of investigations altogether unknown to the 'authorities' of modern Europe. This is certainly not the place for us to enlarge on the subject, but we should at least explain why we say that certain branches of scientific knowledge have a traditional basis, and what we mean by this; and by doing so we shall in fact be showing, still more clearly than we have done so far, what Western science lacks.

We have said that one of the special features of this Western science is its claim to be entirely independent and autonomous; and this claim can only be upheld by systematically ignoring all knowledge of a higher order than scientific knowledge, or better still by formally denying it. What is above science in the necessary hierarchy of knowledge is metaphysics, which is pure and transcendent intellectual knowledge, while by its very definition science is only rational knowledge. Metaphysics is essentially supra-rational; it must be that, or else not be at all. Now rationalism consists, not in simply stating that reason has some value—which only the skeptics contest—but in maintaining that there is nothing above it, or, in other words, that there is no knowledge possible beyond scientific knowledge; thus rationalism necessarily implies the negation of metaphysics. Almost all modern philosophers are rationalists, more or less narrowly and more or less outspokenly. And, among those who are not, there is only sentimentalism and voluntarism, which is no less anti-metaphysical, because having reached this state, if they admit anything other than reason, it is below instead of above reason that they look. True intellectualism is at least as remote from rationalism as modern intuitionism can be, but it is so in exactly the inverse direction. In these circumstances, if a modern philosopher claims to be concerned with metaphysics, one may be sure that what he so names has absolutely nothing in common with true metaphysics, and such is indeed the case. We can only allow these preoccupations the title of 'pseudo-metaphysics', and if nonetheless some valid considerations are occasionally to be found among them, they belong really to the scientific order pure and simple. The general features, then, of characteristically modern thought are these: complete absence of metaphysical knowledge, negation of all knowledge that is not scientific, and arbitrary limitation of scientific knowledge itself to certain particular domains, excluding the rest. Such is the depth of intellectual degradation to which the West has sunk since it left those paths that the rest of mankind follows as a matter of course.

Metaphysics is the knowledge of the universal principles on which all things necessarily depend, directly or indirectly; in the absence of metaphysics, any other knowledge, of whatever order it may be, is literally lacking in principle, and if by that it gains a little in independence (not as a right, but as a matter of fact), it loses much more in scope and depth. That is why Western science is, as it were, all on the surface. While scattering its energies among countless fragments of knowledge, and losing its way among the innumerable details of fact, it learns nothing about the true nature of things, which it declares to be inaccessible in order to justify its powerlessness in this respect; thus its interest is much more practical than speculative. If there are sometimes attempts to unify this eminently analytical learning, they are purely artificial and are never based on anything but more or less wild suppositions; and they all collapse one after the other, until it seems that no scientific theory of any general bearing can last more than half a century at the most. Besides, the Western idea which would make synthesis a sort of result and conclusion of analysis is radically false. The truth is that a synthesis worthy of the name can never be reached by analysis, because one belongs to one order of things and the other to another. By its very nature, analysis may be carried out indefinitely, if its field of action is expansive enough, without one's having got any nearer to a general view over the whole field; it is still less surprising that it should be utterly ineffectual in establishing a connection with principles of a higher order. The analytical character of modern science is shown by the ceaseless growth in the number of 'specialities' the dangers of which August Comte himself could not help pointing out. This 'specialization', so gloried in by certain sociologists under the name of 'division of labor', is the best and surest way of acquiring this 'intellectual shortsightedness' which seems to be among the qualifications demanded of the perfect 'scientist' and without which, moreover, 'scientism' itself would have scarcely any hold. And the 'specialists', once brought outside their own domain, generally show themselves to be unbelievably ingenuous; nothing is easier than to impose on them, and this is what contributes in good part to the success of the most idiotic theories, provided that care is taken to call them 'scientific'. The most idle suppositions, like that of evolution for example, take the rank of 'laws' and are held for proven; and though this success is only temporary, their riddance means that their place has been taken by something else which is always accepted with equal readiness. False syntheses, which are bent on extracting the superior from the inferior (a strange transposition of the conception of democracy), can never be anything more than hypothetical: true synthesis, on the contrary, starting from principles, partakes of their certainty; but it is of course true principles which must be the starting-point, and not mere philosophic assumptions in the manner of Descartes. In short it may be said that science, in disavowing the principles and in refusing to re-attach itself to them, robs itself both of the highest guarantee and of the surest direction that it could have; there is no longer anything valid in it except knowledge of details, and as soon as it seeks to rise one degree higher, it becomes dubious and vacillating. Another consequence of what we have just said about the relations between analysis and synthesis is that the development of science, as the moderns understand it, does not really extend its domain; the amount of fragmentary knowledge may increase indefinitely within this domain, not through deeper penetration, but through division and subdivision carried out always more and more minutely; it is indeed the science of matter and multitude. Besides, even if there should be a real extension, as may happen exceptionally, it would always be within the same order and would not enable this science to rise any higher; in its present state it is separated from its principles by an abyss which, far from being bridgeable, cannot even be made the least little fraction less of an abyss.

When we say that the sciences, even experimental sciences, have in the East a traditional basis, we mean that, unlike Western ones, they are always attached to certain principles; these are never lost sight of, and what is contingent seems only worth studying in that it is a consequence and outward manifestation of something that belongs to a higher order. True, there remains nonetheless a profound distinction between metaphysical knowledge and scientific knowledge, but there is not an absolute discontinuity between them such as is to be noticed in the present state of scientific knowledge in the West. We can take an example even within the Western world, if we consider all the distance that separates the standpoint of ancient and medieval cosmology from that of physics as understood by the moderns; never, until the present epoch, had the study of the sensible world been regarded as self-sufficient; never would the science of this changing and ephemeral multiplicity have been judged truly worthy of the name of knowledge, unless the means had been found of connecting it, in some degree or other, with something stable and permanent. According to the ancient conception, which Easterners have always adhered to, a science was less esteemed for itself than for the degree in which it expressed after its own fashion and represented within a certain order of things a reflection of the higher immutable truth which everything of any reality necessarily partakes of; and, as the features of this truth were incarnated, as it were, in the idea of tradition, all science appeared as an extension of the traditional doctrine itself, as one of its applications, secondary and contingent no doubt, accessory and not essential, constituting an inferior knowledge, but still a true knowledge nonetheless, since it kept a link with that supreme knowledge which belongs to the order of pure intellect. It is clear that this conception is absolutely irreconcilable with the gross practical naturalism which shuts up our contemporaries within the sole domain of contingency—one may even say, to be more exact, within a narrow portion of this domain;[3] and as the Easterners, we repeat, have not varied in this conception and cannot do so without denying the principles on which their civilization is based, the two mentalities appear to be decidedly incompatible. But since it is the West that has changed, and never ceases to change, perhaps a moment will come when its mentality will be modified for the better and become open to a wider understanding, and then this incompatibility will vanish of itself.

3. We say practical naturalism, because this limitation is accepted by people who do not profess naturalism in its more particularly philosophical sense. In just the same way there is a positivist mentality which does not in the least presuppose adherence to positivism as a system.

We think we have shown clearly enough how far the Easterners' appraisal of Western science is justified; and, under these conditions, there is only one thing that can explain the unbounded admiration and superstitious respect that is lavished on this science: this is its perfect harmony with the needs of a purely material civilization. There is, in fact, no question here of disinterested speculation; those minds which are altogether engrossed by outward things are struck by the applications that science gives rise to, and by its above all practical and utilitarian character, and it is especially thanks to the mechanical inventions that the 'scientistic' spirit has had its development. These are the inventions that have aroused, since the beginning of the nineteenth century, a positively delirious enthusiasm, because their objective seems to be the increase of bodily comfort, which is clearly the chief aspiration of the modern world. Moreover, there were thus created unawares in addition more new needs than could be satisfied, so that even from this very relative point of view, progress is most illusory; and, once launched upon this course, it seems no longer possible to stop, as there is always some new want to be supplied. But however that may be, it is these applications, confused with science itself, which more than anything else have made for its credit and prestige. This confusion, which could only arise among people ignorant of what pure speculation is, even in the scientific order, has become so usual that today, on opening no matter what publication, one finds constantly under the name of 'science' what ought properly to be called 'industry'. The typical 'authority' is, in most minds, the engineer, inventor, or constructor of machines. As for scientific theories, they must be considered much more as profiting from this state of mind than as causing it; if those very people who are least capable of understanding them accept them with confidence and receive them as veritable dogma (and the less they understand the more easily they are deluded) it is because they look on them, rightly or wrongly, as closely bound up with these practical inventions which they deem so marvelous. Actually this closeness is much more apparent than real. The more or less inconsistent 'scientistic' hypotheses play no part in these discoveries and these applications, on the interest of which opinions may differ, but which have in any case the merit of being something effective; and, inversely, all that can be realized in the practical order will never prove the truth of any hypothesis. Besides, in a more general way, there could not, properly speaking, be a verification of an hypothesis by experiment, for it is always possible to find several theories which explain equally well the same facts. Certain hypotheses may be eliminated when they are seen to be in contradiction with the facts, but those that are left remain always mere hypotheses and nothing more; this is not the way that certainties could ever be arrived at. However, for men who accept nothing but hard facts, and who have no other criterion of truth than 'experience', by which they simply mean the noticing of sensible phenomena, there can be no question of going further or of proceeding otherwise, and, for such as these, there are only two attitudes possible: either to take one's tone from the realization that scientific theories are hypothetical and to renounce all certainty higher than mere sensible evidence, or, refusing to admit that they are hypothetical, to believe blindly everything that is taught in the name of 'science'. The former attitude, assuredly more intelligent than the latter (always remembering the limitations of 'scientific' intelligence), is that of certain 'authorities' who, being less ingenuous than the others, refuse to be the dupes of their own or their fellows' hypotheses. Thus, except for what is immediately practical, they arrive at a state of more or less complete skepticism, or at least at a sort of probabilism: it is 'agnosticism' no longer applied simply to what goes beyond the domain of science, but extended even to the scientific order itself. They only emerge from this negative attitude by a more or less conscious pragmatism, having regard, like Henri Poincaré, no longer to the truth of a hypothesis but instead to its convenience. Is that not an admission of incurable ignorance? Meanwhile, the second attitude, which may be called dogmatic, is maintained with more or less sincerity by other 'authorities', but especially by those who believe themselves bound for the needs of education to be affirmative: to appear always sure of oneself and of what one says, to cover up difficulties and uncertainties, and never to express anything in a doubtful manner is indeed the easiest way to make sure of being taken seriously and to acquire authority in one's dealings with a public, that is for the most part incompetent and incapable of discernment, whether it is pupils that are being addressed, or whether the task in hand is one of popularization. This same attitude is naturally taken up, and this time with incontestable sincerity, by those who receive such an education. It is also commonly the attitude of what is called 'the man in the street', and the 'scientistic' outlook can be seen in all its fullness, with this characteristic blind belief, among men who have only been semi-educated, in circles reigned over by that mentality which is often qualified as 'primary', although this mentality is not confined to those who have had a 'primary' education.

We spoke just now of 'popularization'. This is another thing altogether peculiar to modern civilization, and in it may be seen one of the chief factors of this state of mind that we are trying to describe. It is one of the forms taken by this strange need for propaganda which animates the Western mind, and which can only be explained by the predominant influence of sentiment. No intellectual consideration justifies proselytism, in which the Easterners see nothing but a proof of ignorance and incomprehension; there is a complete difference between simply expounding the truth as one has understood it, with the one care not to disfigure it, and wishing at any price to make others share one's own conviction. Propaganda and popularization are not even possible except to the detriment of the truth: the pretension of putting it 'within everyone's grasp', of making it accessible to all without distinction, necessarily involves diminishing and deforming it, for it is impossible to admit that all men are equally capable of understanding anything. It is not a question of the greater or lesser extent of education, it is a question of 'intellectual horizon', and that is something which cannot be modified, which is inherent in the very nature of each human individual. The chimerical prejudice of 'equality' goes against all the best established facts, in the intellectual order as well as in the physical order; it is the negation of all natural hierarchy, and it is the debasement of all knowledge to the level of the limited understanding of the masses. People will no longer admit anything that passes common comprehension, and, in fact, the scientific and philosophic conceptions of our epoch are, all told, most lamentably mediocre: modern 'authorities' have succeeded only too well in wiping out all that might have been incompatible with the concern for popularization. Whatever anyone may say, the constitution of any elite cannot be reconciled with the democratic ideal, which demands that one and the same education shall be given to individuals who are most unequally gifted, and who differ widely both in talents and temperament; inevitably the results still continue to vary, in spite of this education, but that is contrary to the intentions of those who instituted it. In any case such a system of teaching is assuredly the most imperfect of all, and the indiscriminate diffusion of scraps of knowledge is always more harmful than beneficial, for it can only bring about a general state of disorder and anarchy. It is such a diffusion that is guarded against by the methods of traditional teaching, as it exists throughout the East, where the very real inconveniences of 'compulsory education' are seen to outweigh by far its imagined benefits. As if it were not already enough that the knowledge available to Westerners contains precious little of the transcendent, even this little is still further diminished in the works of popularization, which only treat of its most inferior aspects, and that too with distortions in order to make them simpler; and these works insist complacently on the most fantastic hypotheses, having the effrontery to give them out as proven truths, and accompanying them with those inept declamations which so please the mob. A half knowledge acquired by such reading, or by an education whose elements are all drawn from hand-books of a like value, is far more injurious than pure and simple ignorance; better for a man to know nothing at all than to have his mind encumbered with false ideas, often ineradicable, especially when they have been inculcated from his earliest years. The ignorant man retains at least the possibility of learning if he is given the opportunity: he may possess a certain natural 'common sense' which, together with the consciousness that he ordinarily has of his own incompetence, is enough to save him from much folly. On the contrary, the man who has been half taught has nearly always a deformed mentality, and what he thinks he knows makes him so self-satisfied that he imagines himself capable of talking about everything, no matter what; he does so at random, and the greater his incompetence the greater his glibness: so simple do all things appear to one who knows nothing!

Besides, even setting aside the evils of popularization itself and considering Western science as a whole and under its most authentic aspects, there remains, in the claim of its promoters to be able to teach it to all without any reserve, a clear sign of mediocrity. In the eyes of the Easterners there can be no great value and no true depth of content in something whose study calls for no particular qualification; and, in fact, Western science is altogether outward and superficial. To characterize it, instead of saying 'ignorant knowledge' we would be willing to say, with very much the same meaning, 'profane knowledge'. There is no real distinction, from this point of view any more than from the others, to be made between philosophy and science. People have sought to define philosophy as 'human wisdom'; indeed it is, but with the strong reserve that it is nothing more than that, a wisdom purely human, in the most limited sense of this word, derived from no element of a higher order than reason; to avoid all uncertainty we would call it also 'profane wisdom', but that amounts to saying that it is not really a wisdom at all, but only the illusory appearance of one. We will not insist here on the consequences of this 'profane' character of all modern Western knowledge; but to show further how superficial and sham this knowledge is, we will call to notice that the methods of teaching in use have the effect of replacing intelligence almost entirely with memory. What is demanded of the pupils, from the time they first go to a primary school to the time they leave the university, is that they should hoard up as much as possible of what is taught them, not that they should assimilate it; those things are especially worked at whose study requires no comprehension; facts are substituted for ideas, and scholarship is commonly mistaken for real knowledge. To promote or to discredit this or that branch of knowledge, this or that method, no more is needed than to declare that it is or is not 'scientific'. What are accounted officially as 'scientific methods' are the most unintelligent methods of learning, methods which exclude everything that is not research after facts for facts' sake down to their most insignificant details; and it is worth noting that the worst abusers under this heading are the 'men of letters'. The prestige of this label 'scientific', even when it is really nothing more than a label, is indeed the triumph of triumphs for the 'scientistic' mind; and as for the respect which is extorted from the masses (including the so-called 'intellectuals') by the use of a simple word, are we not right in calling it 'the superstition of science'?

Of course 'scientistic' propaganda is not carried on only within the West, under the double form of 'compulsory education' and popularization; it is also rife elsewhere, like all the other varieties of Western proselytism. Everywhere that the Europeans have installed themselves, they have wanted to spread these so-called 'benefits of education', always following the same methods, without the least attempt to adapt them and without it entering their heads that there may be already some other kind of education there. Everything that does not come from them is to be considered as null and void, and 'equality' does not allow different peoples and different races to have their own mentality; moreover, the chief 'advantage' that the imposers of this education expect from it is probably, always and everywhere, the blotting out of the traditional outlook. Likewise, once they are away from home, this 'equality' so dear to Westerners amounts to mere uniformity; the rest of what it implies does not come under the category of 'exportable goods' and only concerns the relations between one Westerner and another, for they believe themselves incomparably superior to all other men, among whom they scarcely make any distinctions: the most barbarous black men and the most cultured Easterners are treated in almost the same way, because they are equally outside the one 'civilization' that has the right to exist. Also, the Europeans usually confine themselves to teaching the most rudimentary fragments of all their knowledge. It is not hard to imagine how these fragments must be appreciated by the Easterners, to whom even what is highest in this knowledge would seem chiefly remarkable for its narrowness, and stamped with a rather gross ingenuousness. As the peoples who have a civilization of their own prove themselves on the whole refractory to this so much boasted education, while the peoples without culture submit to it much more docilely, Westerners are perhaps not far from judging the latter superior to the former; they are prepared to show at least a relative esteem for those whom they look on as susceptible of 'rising' to their level, even though this elevation be considered only possible after some centuries of the regime of compulsory elementary education have passed. Unfortunately, however, what the people of the West call 'rising' would be called by some, as far as they are concerned, 'sinking'; that is what all true Easterners think, even if they do not say so, and if they prefer, as most often happens, to hedge themselves round with the most disdainful silence, leaving, so little does it matter to them, Western vanity free to interpret their attitude as it pleases.

The Europeans have so high an opinion of their science that they believe its prestige to be irresistible, and they imagine that the other peoples must fall down in admiration before their most insignificant discoveries; this state of mind, which leads them sometimes into strange misunderstandings, is not altogether new, and we have found a rather amusing example of it in Leibnitz. This philosopher, as is known, had planned to establish what he called a 'universal characteristic', that is a sort of generalized algebra, made applicable to the notions of every order, instead of being limited to quantitative notions alone; moreover, this idea had been inspired in him by certain authors of the Middle Ages, especially Raymond Lull and Trithemius. In the course of the studies which he made toward realizing this project, Leibnitz came to be engrossed with the meaning of the ideographic characters that constitute Chinese writing, and more particularly with the symbolical figures which form the basis of the *I Ching*. It will be seen how he understood these last: 'Leibnitz,' says Couturat,

> believed he had found by his binary numeration (a numeration which only employs the signs 0 and 1 and in which he saw the image of creation *ex nihilo*) the interpretation of the characters of Fu Hsi, mysterious and most ancient Chinese symbols, whose meaning was unknown to the European missionaries and to the Chinese themselves.... He proposed to use this interpretation for the propaganda of the Faith in China, seeing that it was fit to give the Chinese a high idea of European science, and to show the accord of this science with the venerable and sacred traditions of Chinese wisdom. He added this interpretation to the exposition of his binary arithmetic which he sent to the Paris Academy of Sciences.[4]

---

4. Leibnitz, *La Logique*, pp 474–475.

Here, in fact, is the text of the thesis in question:

> What is surprising in this calculus (of binary arithmetic) is that this arithmetic by 0 and 1 happens to contain the mystery of the lines of an ancient king and philosopher named Fohy, who is believed to have lived more than four thousand years ago[5] and whom the Chinese regard as the founder of their Empire and of their sciences. There are several linear figures which are attributed to him, and they are all the outcome of this arithmetic; but it is enough to give here the Figure of eight Cova,[6] as it is called, which passes for fundamental, and to add the explanation, which is clear so long as it be noticed first of all that a whole line signifies unity or 1, and secondly, that a broken line signifies zero or 0. It is perhaps more than a thousand years since the Chinese lost the meaning of the Cova or Lineations of Fohy, and they have made commentaries about it, in which they have sought to give I know not what far-fetched interpretations, so that they have now had to receive the true one from the Europeans. This is how: it is scarcely more than two years since I sent to the Rev. Father Bouvet, a celebrated French Jesuit living at Peking, my way of counting by 0 and 1, and it needed no more to make him realize that it is the key to the figures of Fohy. So, writing to me on November 17, 1701, he sent me this philosopher-prince's great figure, which goes up to 64,[7] and leaves no longer any room for doubting the truth of our interpretation, so that one may say that this Father has deciphered the enigma of Fohy with the aid of what I had communicated to him. And as these figures are perhaps the most

---

5. The exact date is 3468 BC, according to a chronology based on the precise description of the state of the heavens at that epoch; it should be added that actually the name Fu Hsi serves to designate a whole period of Chinese history.

6. *K'ua* is the Chinese name for 'trigrams', that is figures obtained by assembling in threes, with every possible combination, whole and broken straight lines. Actually the number of figures so obtainable is eight.

7. This reference is to the sixty-four 'hexagrams' of Wen-Wang, that is figures of six lines formed by combining the eight 'trigrams' two by two. Incidentally, Leibnitz's interpretation is quite incapable of explaining, among other things, why these 'hexagrams', as well as the 'trigrams' that they are derived from, are always tabulated in *circular* form.

ancient monument of science in the world, this restitution of their meaning, after so great an interval of time, will seem all the more curious.... And this accord gives me a high opinion of the depth of Fohy's meditations. For what we now find easy was not all so in those remote times.... And as it is believed in China that Fohy is as well the author of the Chinese characters, although they have been much changed by the lapse of time, his essay in Arithmetic leads one to judge that there might well be something else of import there in relation to numbers and to ideas, if the foundation of Chinese writing could be laid bare, the more so as it is believed in China that he had regard to numbers in establishing it. The Rev. Father Bouvet is much inclined to press this point, and very capable of succeeding in many respects. However, I know not if there has ever been in Chinese writing an advantage approaching that which should necessarily be in a Characteristic that I am planning. This is that all reasoning which may be deduced from notions, might be deduced from their characters by a manner of calculation, which would be one of the chief means of aiding the human mind.[8]

We were anxious to reproduce at length this curious document, by means of which one may measure the limits in understanding of the man whom we nonetheless regard as the most 'intelligent' of all the modern philosophers. Leibnitz was convinced in advance that his 'Characteristic', which moreover he never succeeded in constituting (and the 'logicians' of today are scarcely more advanced), could not fail to be very superior to the Chinese ideography; and the best of all is that he thinks to do Fu Hsi great honor in attributing to him an

---

8. 'Explication de l'Arithmétique binaire, qui se sert des seuls caractères 0 et 1, avec des remarques sur son utilité, et sur ce qu'elle donne le sens des anciennes figures chinoises de Fohy', *Memoires de l'Académie des Sciences*, 1907 (*Oeuvres mathématiques de Leibnitz*, ed. Gerhardt, t. VII, pp 226–227. See also *De Dyadicis*: ibid., t. VII, pp 223–234. This text ends as follows: *Ita mirum accidit, ut res ante ter et amplius (millia?) annos nota in extremo nostri continentis oriente, nunc in extremo ejus occidente, sed melioribus ut spero auspiis resuscitaretur. Nam non apparet, ante usum hujus characterismi ad augendam numerorum scientiam innotuisse. Sinenses vero ipsi ne Arithmeticam quidem rationem intelligentes nescio quos mysticos significatus in characteribus mere numeralibus sibi fingebant.*

'essay in arithmetic' and the first idea of his own little play on numbers. We seem to see here the smile of the Chinese, if they had been presented with this rather puerile interpretation, which would have been very far from giving them 'a high idea of European science,' but which would have been fit to make them realize very exactly its actual range. The truth is that the Chinese have never 'lost the meaning,' or rather the meanings, of the symbols in question; only they do not feel themselves in the least obliged to explain them to the first-comer, especially if they judge that it would be a waste of breath; and Leibnitz, in speaking of 'I know not what far-fetched interpretations' admits in so many words that he understands nothing about it. It is just these interpretations, carefully preserved by the tradition (which the commentaries never cease to follow faithfully), that constitute 'the true one', and moreover there is here no 'mystery'; but what better proof of incomprehension could be given than the taking of metaphysical symbols for 'purely numerical characters'? They are, in fact, essentially metaphysical symbols, these 'trigrams' and 'hexagrams', a synthetic representation of theories that are susceptible of unlimited developments, susceptible also of multiple adaptations, if, instead of keeping to the domain of the principles, one wishes to apply them to one or another determined order of things. Leibnitz would have been most surprised if he had been told that his arithmetical interpretation was also included among these meanings which he rejected without knowing, but only on an altogether accessory and subordinate level; for this interpretation is not false in itself, and it is perfectly compatible with all the others, but it is quite incomplete and insufficient, even insignificant when considered by itself, and may only be deemed interesting in virtue of the analogical correspondence which connects the lower meanings with the higher one, in accordance with what we have said about the nature of the 'traditional sciences'. The higher meaning is the pure metaphysical meaning; as for the rest, they are only different applications, more or less important, but always contingent. It is in this way that there may be an arithmetical application, just as there are an indefinite number of others, just as there is for example a logical application, which might have better served Leibnitz's project had he had been aware of it, just as there is a social application, which is the basis of Confucianism, just as there is an astronomical application, the only one that the Japanese have ever been able to grasp,[9] and just as there is even a divinatory application, which the Chinese moreover look on as one of the lowest of all, and the practice of which they leave to the wandering jugglers. If Leibnitz had been in direct contact with the Chinese, they might have explained to him (but would he have understood?) that even the numbers which he used might symbolize ideas of an order much more profound than the order of mathematics, and that it is by reason of such a symbolism that numbers played a part in the formation of the ideograms, no less than in the expression of the Pythagorean doctrines (which shows that these things were not unknown to the ancients of the West). The Chinese might even have accepted the notation by 0 and 1, and have taken these 'purely numerical characters' to represent symbolically the metaphysical ideas of *yin* and of *yang* (which have moreover nothing to do with the conception of the creation *ex nihilo*), there being nonetheless many reasons for them to prefer, as more adequate, the representation furnished by Fu Hsi's 'lineations', of which the essential and direct object is in the domain of metaphysics. We have treated this example at length because it illustrates clearly the difference that exists between philosophical systematization and traditional synthesis, between Western science and Eastern wisdom; it is not hard to see, judging from this example—which also serves as a symbol—on which side lie the incomprehension and the narrowness of outlook.[10] Leibnitz, in his pretension to understand the Chinese symbols better than the Chinese themselves, is a veritable forerunner of the orientalists, who—the Germans above all—have the same pretension with regard to all

9. The French translation of the *I Ching* by Philastre (*Annales du Musée Guimet*; vols. VIII and XXIII), which is moreover an extremely remarkable work, has the fault of considering rather too exclusively the astronomical meaning.

10. We will recall here what we said of the plurality of meanings of all traditional texts, and especially of the Chinese ideograms in *Introduction to the Study of the Hindu Doctrines*, pt 2, chap. 9. We will add also this quotation borrowed from Philastre: 'In Chinese, a word (or a character) scarcely ever has an absolutely defined and limited meaning; the meaning results very generally from the position in the sentence, but above all from its use in some older book or other, and from its accepted interpretation in this case.... A word has no value except through its traditional acceptations.' (*I Ching*, pt 1, p 8.)

the conceptions and all the doctrines of the East, and who refuse to take into the least consideration the opinion of the authorized representatives of these doctrines: we have mentioned elsewhere the case of Deussen thinking to explain Shankarāchārya to the Hindus, and interpreting him through the ideas of Schopenhauer; these are indeed manifestations of one and the same mentality.

There is still a last remark that we should make with regard to this: it is that Westerners, who advertise so insolently on every occasion belief in their own superiority and in that of their science, are really very much beside the mark when they call Eastern wisdom 'arrogant', as some of them do at times, on the grounds that it does not submit to the limitations that they are used to, and because they cannot make allowance for what goes beyond these limitations. This is one of the habitual faults of mediocrity, and it is mediocrity which forms the basis of the democratic spirit. Arrogance, in reality, is something very Western; so also, moreover, is humility, and, however much of a paradox that may seem, these two opposites go rather closely together: it is an example of the duality which dominates the whole order of sentiment and which is proved most obviously by the innate character of moral conceptions, for the notions of good and evil could not exist but by their very opposition. In actual fact, arrogance and humility are equally strange to Eastern wisdom (we might as well say to wisdom without epithet) and leave it equally unaffected, because in essence it is purely intellectual, and entirely detached from all sentimentality; it knows that the human being is at the same time much less and much more than it is believed to be by the people of the West, at least by those of the present day, and it also knows that it is just what it should be to occupy the place assigned to it in the order of the universe. Man, that is, human individuality, by no means holds a privileged or exceptional place, either one way or the other; he is neither at the top nor at the bottom of the scale of beings: he represents simply, in the hierarchy of existence, a state like the others, among an indefinitude of others, many of which are above him, and many of which also are below him. It is not hard to show, even in this respect, that humility goes very readily hand in hand with a certain kind of arrogance: it is just in seeking to abase man, as they often do in the West, that they find the means of attributing to him at the same time a really quite undue importance, at least insofar as his individuality is concerned; perhaps it is an example of that kind of unconscious hypocrisy, which is, in one degree or another, inseparable from all 'moralism', and in which the Easterners see fairly generally one of the specific marks of the Westerner. Besides, this counterbalancing humility by no means always exists. There is also, among a good number of other Westerners, a veritable deification of human reason, worshipping itself either directly or through the science which is its work; it is the most extreme form of rationalism and of 'scientism', but it is their most natural outcome and altogether the most logical one. Indeed, anyone who knows nothing beyond this science and this reason may well have the illusion of their absolute supremacy; anyone who knows nothing superior to humanity, and more particularly to this type of humanity which is represented by the modern West, may be tempted to deify it, especially if sentimentalism intrudes (and we have shown that it is far from being incompatible with rationalism). All this is only the inevitable consequence of ignorance of the principles, an ignorance which we have denounced as the capital vice of Western science; and, despite Littré's protestations, we do not think that Auguste Comte caused the slightest deviation in positivism by wishing to set up a 'religion of humanity'; this particular 'mysticism' was nothing more than an attempt to fuse the two characteristic tendencies of the modern civilization. Worse still, there exists even a materialist pseudo-mysticism: we have known people who went so far as to declare that even if they should have no rational motive for being materialists, they would nonetheless continue to be so, solely because it is 'finer' to 'do good' without any hope of possible recompense. These people, whose minds are so powerfully influenced by 'moralism' (and their morality, in spite of calling itself 'scientific', is at bottom nonetheless purely sentimental), are naturally among those who profess the 'religion of science'. As this, in all truth, can only be a 'pseudo-religion', we deem it far juster to call it a 'superstition of science': a belief which is only based on ignorance (even if it is that of 'authority') and on vain prejudice does not deserve to be looked at in any other way than as a common superstition.

3

THE SUPERSTITION
OF LIFE

AMONG THE MANY THINGS that Westerners often blame the Eastern civilizations for are their fixity and stability; these characteristics amount in their eyes to a denial of progress, which indeed they are, as we readily admit; but to see a fault in this, one must believe in progress. For us, these characteristics show that these civilizations partake of the immutability of the principles upon which they are based, and that is one of the essential aspects of the idea of tradition. It is because the modern civilization is lacking in principle that it is eminently unstable. Besides, one should not imagine that the stability we speak of goes to the length of excluding all change; what it does is to reduce the change to being never more than an adaptation to circumstances, by which the principles are not in the least affected, and which may on the contrary be strictly deduced from them, if they are resorted to, not for themselves, but in view of a definite application; and that is the point of all the 'traditional sciences', apart from metaphysics which, as knowledge of the principles, is self-sufficing, for these sciences cover the range of all that may happen to proceed from the principles, including social institutions. It would also be wrong to confuse immutability with immobility; such misunderstandings are common among Westerners because they are generally incapable of separating conception from imagination, and because their minds are inextricably bound up with representations dictated by the senses; this is very obvious in such philosophers as Kant, who cannot however be ranked among the 'sensualists'. The immutable is not what is contrary to change, but what is above it; just as the 'supra-rational' is not the 'irrational'. There is every reason for distrusting the tendency to arrange things in artificial oppositions and antitheses, by an interpretation which is both systematic and falsely simple, arising chiefly from the inability to go further and resolve the apparent contrasts in the harmonious unity of a true synthesis. It is nonetheless true that there is very real opposition, from the point of view that we have in mind here as well as from many others, between East and West, at least as things are at present: there is divergence, but it should not be forgotten that this divergence is one-sided and not symmetrical, being like that of a branch which grows away from the trunk; it is the civilization of the West alone which, by going in the direction that it has followed throughout the last centuries, has become so remote from the civilizations of the East that between it and them there seems to be, as it were, no longer any common element, any term of comparison, or any meeting-ground for agreement and reconciliation.

The Westerner, or rather the modern Westerner (it is always the latter that we mean), shows himself to be essentially changeable and inconstant, as if vowed to ceaseless movement and agitation, and, what is more, to have no ambition to emerge from it; in a word, his plight is that of a being who is unable to find his balance, but who, in his inability to do so, will not admit that the thing is possible in itself or even desirable, going so far as to make his own impotence something to boast of. These changes which he is subject to and which he takes delight in without requiring that they should lead him to any end, because he has come to like them for their own sake, constitute in fact what he calls 'progress', as if it were enough simply to walk, quite regardless of direction, to be sure of advancing. As for the goal of his advance, he does not even dream of asking himself what it is; and the scattering of his forces amid the multiplicity which is the inevitable consequence of these changes without principle and without aim, and indeed the only consequence whose reality cannot be contested, he calls 'being enriched': that is yet another word which, in the gross materialism of the image that it calls up, is altogether typical and representative of the modern mentality. The need for outward activity carried to such a pitch, together with the love of effort for effort's sake, independent of the results that can be got by it, is not at all natural to man, at least not to the normal man, according to the idea which has always and everywhere been accepted of him; but it has become in a sense natural to the Westerner, perhaps as a result of habit, which Aristotle says is like a second nature, but above all through the atrophy of the being's higher faculties, which goes necessarily with the intensive development of the lower elements. A man without means of extricating himself from agitation has nothing left but to be satisfied with it, just as a man whose intelligence stops short at rational activity finds such activity admirable and sublime; to be fully at ease in a limited sphere, whatever it may be, one must be blind to the possibility of there being anything beyond. The aspirations of the Westerner, alone of all mankind (we are not considering the savages, about whom it is, moreover, very difficult to know what to think), are as a rule strictly confined to the sensible world and to its dependencies, among which we include the whole order of feeling and a good part of the order of reason; no doubt there are praiseworthy exceptions, but we can only consider here the general and common mentality, such as is truly characteristic of the place and the period.

Another strange phenomenon may be noted in the intellectual domain itself, or rather in what is left of it, and this, which is only a particular case of the state of mind that we have just described, is the passion for research taken as an end in itself, quite regardless of seeing it terminate in any solution. While the rest of mankind seeks for the sake of finding and of knowing, the Westerner of today seeks for the sake of seeking; the Gospel saying, 'Seek and ye shall find,' is a dead letter for him, in the full force of this phrase, since he calls 'death' anything and everything that constitutes a definite finality, just as he gives the name 'life' to what is no more than fruitless agitation. This unhealthy taste for research, real 'mental restlessness' without end and without issue, shows itself at its very plainest in modern philosophy, the greater part of which represents no more than a series of quite artificial problems, which only exist because they are badly propounded, owing their origin and survival to nothing but carefully kept up verbal confusions; they are problems which, considering how they are formulated, are truly insoluble, but, on the other hand, no one is in the least anxious to solve them, and they were created simply that they might go on indefinitely feeding controversies and discussions which lead nowhere, and which are not meant to lead anywhere. This substituting research for knowledge (and closely bound up with it is the remarkable abuse which consists in 'theories of knowledge' to which we have already called attention) is simply giving up the proper object of intelligence, and it is scarcely strange that in these conditions some people have come ultimately to suppress the very idea of truth, for the truth can only be conceived of as the end to be reached, and these people want no end to their research. It follows that there can be nothing intellectual in their efforts, even taking intelligence in its widest, not in its highest and purest sense; and if we have been able to speak of a 'passion for research', it is in fact because sentiment has intruded into domains where it ought never to have set foot. Of course we are not protesting against the actual existence of sentiment, which is a natural fact, but only against its abnormal and illegitimate extension; one must know how to put each thing in its place and leave it there, but this calls for an understanding of the universal order, which is beyond the reach of the modern world, where disorder is law. To denounce sentimentalism is not to deny sentiment any more than to denounce rationalism amounts to denying reason; sentimentalism and rationalism are both nothing more than the results of abuses, although the modern West sees them as the two extremes of an alternative from which it cannot escape.

We have already said that sentiment is quite close to the material world; it is not for nothing that the sensible and the sentimental are so closely linked by language, and, although they are not to be altogether confused with one another, they are only two modes of one and the same order of things. The modern mind faces almost exclusively outward, toward the world of the senses; sentiment seems inward to it, and it often seeks, in virtue of this, to oppose sentiment to sensation; but that is all very relative; and the truth is that the psychologist's 'introspection' itself grasps nothing but phenomena, or, in other words, outward and superficial modifications of the being; there is nothing truly inward and deep except the higher part of the intelligence. This will seem surprising to those who, like the intuitionists of today, only know intelligence in its lower part, represented by the sensible faculties and by reason insofar as it turns its attention to the objects of sense, and believe it to be more outward than sentiment; but, in relation to the transcendent intellectuality of the Easterners, rationalism and intuitionism go closely together upon one and the same plane, and both stop short at the being's 'exterior', despite the illusions by which either conception believes that it grasps something of the being's interior nature. But when all is said and done, in neither of them is there ever any question of going beyond sensible things; they disagree simply on the methods to be put into practice for reaching these things, on how they are to be considered, and on which of their diverse aspects should come most to the fore: we might say that the ones prefer to insist on the 'matter' side, the others on the 'life' side. These are, in fact, the limitations which Western thought cannot throw off: the Greeks were unable to free themselves from form; modern Westerners seem above all powerless to extricate themselves from matter, and, when they try to do so, they cannot in any case get away from the domain of life. All these, life just as much as matter and even more so than form, are merely conditions of existence particular to the sensible world, so that they are all on one same plane, as we have just been saying. The modern West, save for exceptional cases, takes the sensible world as the sole object of knowledge; whether it prefers to attach itself to one or to the other of this world's conditions, or whether it studies it from this or that point of view, scouring it in no matter what direction, the domain in which its mind works continues nonetheless to be always the same. If this domain appears to become at all enlarged, it never does so to any real extent, even supposing that the appearance is not altogether illusory. There are moreover, bordering on the sensible world, various prolongations which also belong to the same degree of universal existence. According to whether a man has in mind this or that condition, among those which define this world, he may at times reach one or another of these prolongations, but he will remain nonetheless shut up in a special and determined domain. When Bergson says that the natural object of intelligence is matter, he is wrong in giving the name intelligence to what he means, and he does so through his ignorance of what is truly intellectual; but he is substantially right if, by this faulty designation, he means no more than the lowest part of the intelligence, or, to be more precise, the use that is commonly made of it in the West of today. As for him, it is clearly and essentially to life that he attaches himself: the part played by 'élan vital' in his theories is well known, as is also the meaning he gives to what he calls 'pure duration'; but life, whatever 'value' be attributed to it, is nonetheless inextricably bound up with matter, and it is always the same world that is being considered here, whether it is looked at with the eyes of an 'organicist' or 'vitalist' or, on the other hand, with those of a 'mechanist'. Only, when, of the elements which make up this world, the vital element is held to be more important than the material one, it is natural that sentiment should take precedence over so-called intelligence; the intuitionists with their 'mental contortions', the pragmatists with their 'inner experience', simply address themselves to the dark powers of instinct and sentiment, which they take for the being's very depth, and, when they follow their thought or rather their tendency to its conclusion, they end, like William James, in proclaiming the supremacy of the 'subconscious', by the most incredible subversion of the natural order ever chronicled in the history of ideas.

Life, considered in itself, is always full of change and ceaseless modification; it is, then, understandable that it should hold such fascinating sway over the outlook of the modern civilization, whose changefulness is also its most striking characteristic, obvious at first sight, even if one stops short at an altogether superficial examination. When a man is imprisoned like this in life and in the conceptions directly connected with it, he can know nothing about what escapes change, about the transcendent and immutable order, which is that of the universal principles; in this case there can no longer be any possibility of metaphysical knowledge, and we are always brought round again to this same conclusive statement of fact, which is the inevitable consequence of each of the modern West's characteristics. We say here change rather than movement, because the former word is wider in scope than the latter: movement is only the physical or rather the mechanical modality of change, and there are conceptions which have in view other modalities that cannot be brought under the heading of movement, and which even hold these modalities to be more strictly 'vital' in character to the exclusion of movement in its ordinary sense, that is, as meaning just a change of position. There again, it would be wrong to exaggerate certain oppositions, since they only appear as such from a more or less limited point of view: for example, a mechanistic theory is, by definition, a theory that claims to explain everything by matter and movement; but if the idea of life were given its widest possible extension, movement itself could be made to fit into it, and it would be seen that the so-called opposed or antagonistic theories are, at bottom, much more equivalent than their respective partisans will admit;[1] there is scarcely any difference between the two except for a little more or a little less narrowness of outlook. In any case, a conception that gives itself out as a 'philosophy of life' is necessarily, then and there, a 'philosophy of becoming'; we mean that it is confined to this state, and cannot escape from it (to become and to change being synonymous), which leads it to situate all reality therein and to deny anything whatever outside or beyond it, since the systematic mind is so framed as to imagine that it comprises within its formulas the whole of the Universe; that is yet another formal negation of metaphysics. One such, among others, is evolutionism in all its forms, from the most mechanistic conceptions, including gross 'transformism', to theories like Bergson's; there is no room to be found there for anything except the state of becoming, and even then, strictly speaking, it is only a more or less limited part of this state that is kept in view. Evolution, all told, is nothing but change, backed up by an illusion with regard to the direction and quality of this change; evolution and progress are one and the same thing, to all intents and purposes, but the former term is often preferred today because it seems to give the impression of being more 'scientific'. Evolutionism is, as it were, a product of those two great modern superstitions, that of science and that of life, and its success

---

1. This corresponds to what we once said about the two conflicting varieties of 'monism', the one spiritualistic and the other materialistic.

is made for the very reason that both rationalism and sentimentalism find full satisfaction in it; the variable proportions in which these two tendencies are combined account very largely for the diversity of forms in which this theory is clothed. The evolutionists see change everywhere, even in God himself when they admit him: Bergson is no exception when he imagines God as 'a center from which worlds shoot out, and which is not a *thing* but a continuity of shooting out'; and he added expressly: 'God thus defined has nothing of the already made; he is unceasing life, action, freedom.'[2] It is, then, nothing more nor less than these ideas of life and of action which our contemporaries are literally obsessed with, and which, as in the above case, intrude themselves into a domain that seeks to be speculative; in other words they suppress speculation in the interests of action, which encroaches everywhere and absorbs everything. This conception of a God in a state of becoming, who is only immanent and not transcendent, together with that (which amounts to the same) of a truth in the making, which is nothing more than a sort of ideal limit, devoid of all present reality, is by no means exceptional in modern thought; the pragmatists, who have adopted the idea of a limited God for chiefly 'moralist' motives, are not its original inventors, since what is held to develop must necessarily be conceived of as limited. Pragmatism, by its very name, poses above all as a 'philosophy of action'; its more or less avowed assumption is that man only has needs of a practical order, material ones and, together with these, sentimental ones. It means, then, the doing away with intellectuality; but, if this is so, why go on wanting to evolve theories? That is rather hard to understand; and if pragmatism, like skepticism, which it only differs from with regard to action, wished to conform to its own standards, it would have to limit itself to a mere mental attitude, which it cannot even seek to justify logically without giving itself the lie; but there is no doubt that it is very difficult to keep strictly within such bounds. However degraded a man may be intellectually, he cannot at least help reasoning, if only in order to deny reason; moreover the pragmatists do not deny it as the skeptics do, but they seek to reduce it to serving purely practical

---

2. *Creative Evolution*, p 262.

ends; as the followers of those who sought to reduce the whole of intelligence to reason, though without denying it a theoretic function, they have gone one degree lower in the scale of degradation. There is even one point where the pragmatists carry their denying further than the pure skeptics: the latter do not contest the existence of truth outside us, but only our ability to reach it; the pragmatists, in imitation of one or two Greek sophists (who very probably did not take themselves seriously), go to the lengths of suppressing truth itself.

Life and action go closely together; the one's domain is also the other's, and it is to this limited domain that the whole Western civilization keeps, today more than ever. Elsewhere we have told what view the Easterners take of the limitations of action and its consequences, and how for them, in this respect, knowledge is the opposite of action: the Far-Eastern theory of 'non-action' and the Hindu theory of 'deliverance' are inaccessible to the ordinary Western mind, which cannot conceive that a man may dream of freeing himself from action, still less that he may actually come to do so. Besides, action is not generally considered except in its most outward forms, in those that strictly correspond to physical movement: hence this growing desire for speed and this feverish restlessness so peculiar to modern life; it is all action for the pleasure of action, and this can only be called agitation, for even in action there are certain degrees to observe and certain distinctions to make. Nothing would be easier than to show how incompatible this is with all that concerns reflection and concentration, or in other words with the essential means of all true knowledge; it is indeed the triumph of dispersion, in the most complete turning of all things inside out that can be conceived; it means the definite ruin of whatever may still be left of intellectuality, if nothing comes to react in time against these fatal tendencies. Fortunately, such an excess of evil may bring on a reaction, and even the physical dangers inherent in so abnormal a development may end by inspiring a salutary dread. Besides, the very fact that the domain of action only admits of very limited possibilities, even if it may seem to do otherwise, makes it impossible that this development should go on indefinitely, and sooner or later the nature of things will forcibly impose a change of direction. But for the moment we do not intend to consider the possibilities of a future that is perhaps remote. What we have in view is the present state of the West, and all that we see of it is clear confirming evidence that material progress and intellectual decadence are knit closely together; we have no wish to decide which of the two is the cause or effect of the other, especially as we are dealing, in the main, with a complex whole in which the relations of the different elements are sometimes reciprocal and alternating. Without trying to trace the modern world back to its beginnings and to study the way in which its special mentality may have been formed, as we should have to do if the question were to be fully disposed of, we can say this much: there must have been already a depreciation and a dwindling of intellectuality for material progress to become important enough to overstep certain bounds; but once this movement had started, with the concerns of material progress absorbing little by little all man's faculties, intellectuality went on growing gradually weaker and weaker, until it reached the plight that we see it in today, with perhaps a still worse one in store for it, although that certainly seems difficult. On the other hand, the expansion of sentimentality is by no means incompatible with material progress, because the two are, fundamentally, things of almost the same order; we shall be excused for coming back to this point so often, since, unless it is understood, we cannot grasp what is going on around us. This expansion of sentimentality, corresponding to the regress of intellectuality, will be all the more excessive and disordered for not meeting anything that might effectively check it or direct it, since this part could certainly not be played by 'scientism', which, as we have seen, is far from being immune to sentimental contagion, and which offers no more than a false semblance of intellectuality.

One of the most noticeable symptoms of the preponderance acquired by sentimentality is what we call 'moralism', which is the clearly marked tendency to refer everything to concerns of a moral order, or at least to subordinate everything else to them, especially what is considered as coming within the domain of intelligence. Morality in itself is something essentially sentimental; it represents as relative and contingent a point of view as possible, and one, moreover, that has never been held except by the West; but 'moralism', in the already defined sense of the word, is an exaggeration of this point of view, and only came into being quite recently. A moral code, whatever foundation is given it, and whatever importance is attributed to it, is not and cannot be anything more than a rule of action. For men who are no longer interested in anything but action it is clear that morality must figure very largely indeed, and they attach themselves to it all the more because considerations of this order may be made to pass for thought in a period of intellectual decadence. It is this that explains the birth of 'moralism'. Something of the kind had already come to light toward the end of the Greek civilization, but without growing, as far as one can tell, to the proportions which it has taken on in our time; in fact, from Kant onward, almost all modern philosophy has been saturated with 'moralism', which amounts to saying that it gives precedence to the practical over the speculative, the former being moreover considered from a special angle; this tendency reached its full development with the philosophies of life and of action that we have spoken of. On the other hand we have mentioned the obsession, which haunts even the most avowed materialists, of what are called 'scientific morals', which represent exactly the same tendency; it may be called scientific or philosophical according to individual tastes, but it is never any more than an expression of sentimentality, and this expression does not even vary to any appreciable extent. Indeed, a curious thing about it all is that the moral conceptions within any given sphere of society are all extraordinarily alike, in spite of their claim to be based on considerations that are different and sometimes even conflicting. This is what shows up the artificiality of the theories by which each man strives to justify certain practical rules, which are always the ones commonly observed about him. All told, these theories simply represent the particular preferences of those who formulate or adopt them. Often a party interest plays no small role as well. As proof of this no more is needed than the way in which 'lay morals' (it matters little whether they are called scientific or philosophical) are put in opposition to religious morals. Besides, as the moral point of view only exists for social reasons and no other, the intrusion of politics into the same domain is not to be unduly wondered at; it is perhaps less shocking than the utilization for similar ends of theories that are made out to be purely scientific; but, after all, has not the 'scientistic' mentality itself been created to serve certain political interests? We doubt very much whether most champions of evolutionism are altogether innocent of any such hidden motive, and, to take another example, the so-called 'science of religions' is much more like a weapon of controversy than a serious science; these are among the cases that we have already alluded to, cases where rationalism is chiefly a mask for sentimentality.

It is not only among the 'scientists' and among the philosophers that the encroachment of 'moralism' may be noticed; notice must also be taken, in this respect, of the degeneration of the religious idea, such as it is found to be in the innumerable sects that have sprung from Protestantism. These are the only forms of religion which are specifically modern, and they are characterized by a progressive reduction of the doctrinal element in the interests of the moral or sentimental element; this phenomenon is a particular instance of the general diminishing of intellectuality, and it is no mere chance that the epoch of the Reformation coincides with that of the Renaissance, that is, precisely with the beginning of the modern period. In certain branches of contemporary Protestantism the doctrine has dwindled into nothing at all, and, as the worship, in a parallel way, has also been reduced to practically nothing, the moral element is ultimately all that is left: 'Liberal Protestantism' is no more than a 'moralism' with a religious label; it cannot be said that it is still a religion in the strict sense of the word, because, of the three elements that enter into the definition of religion, there remains no more than one alone. Having reached this stage, it should rather be classed as a sort of special philosophical way of thinking; besides, its representatives are by and large in sympathy with the champions of 'lay morals', which are also styled independent, and they have even been known on occasion to associate themselves openly with them, which shows that they are conscious of their real affinities. As a name for things of this kind, we willingly use the word 'pseudo-religion'; and we apply also this same word to all the 'neo-spiritualist' sects, which are born and prosper above all in the Protestant countries, because 'Neo-Spiritualism' and 'Liberal

Protestantism' spring from the same tendencies and from the same state of mind. The place of religion, owing to the suppression of the intellectual element (or its absence in the case of new creations), is taken by religiosity, or, in other words, by a mere sentimental aspiration, more or less vague and inconsistent; and this religiosity is to religion just about what the shadow is to the body. Here can be seen traces of the 'religious experience' of William James (which is further complicated by its appeal to the 'subconscious'), and also the 'inner life' in the sense which the modernists give it, for modernism was nothing but an attempt to introduce the mentality in question into Catholicism itself, an attempt that was broken against the force of the traditional outlook, whose sole refuge, in the modern West, appears to be Catholicism, save for individual exceptions which may always exist apart from all organization.

It is among the Anglo-Saxon peoples that 'moralism' rages with its greatest intensity, and it is there too that the love of action may be seen in its most extreme forms, which shows that these two things are indeed closely knit together, as we have said. There is a strange irony in the current conception of the English as being a people essentially attached to tradition, and those who think so are quite simply confusing tradition with custom. The ease with which certain words come to be misused is truly extraordinary: there are some who have gone so far as to give the name 'traditions' to popular habits, or even to conventions of quite recent origin, without importance or real significance. As for ourselves, we refuse to give this name to what is only a more or less automatic respect for certain outward forms, which are sometimes nothing more than 'superstitions' in the etymological sense of the word. True tradition dwells in the outlook of a people or race or civilization, and it springs from causes that lie far deeper. The Anglo-Saxon outlook is in reality quite as anti-traditional as the French and Germanic outlooks, but in what seems to be rather a different way, for in Germany it is more the tendency of 'scientism' that predominates and the French tend more toward scholarship. Little matter, however, whether it is 'moralism' or the 'scientistic' attitude that prevails, for it would, we repeat once again, be artificial to seek to separate entirely these two tendencies, which represent the two sides of the modern outlook, and which are to be found in varying proportions among all the peoples of the West. It seems that today the 'moralist' tendency has fairly generally the upper hand, though it is only a few years since the domination of 'scientism' was the more marked; but the one's gain is not necessarily the other's loss, since the two can be very well reconciled, and, in spite of all fluctuations, the common mind links them fairly closely together: it has room, at one and the same time, for all those idols that we spoke of earlier. However, a sort of crystallization of the different anti-traditional elements of the modern outlook is now taking place rather with the idea of 'life', and what goes with it, as center, just as a similar crystallization took place in the nineteenth century round about the idea of 'science', and in the eighteenth about that of 'reason'. We speak of ideas, but we should do better simply to speak of words, since all this is a triumph of the hypnotic power of mere words. What is sometimes called 'ideology', with an unfavorable implication by those who are not its dupes (for in spite of everything there are still one or two to be met with who remain undeluded), is really nothing more than verbalism, and in this connection we can take up again the word 'superstition' in the etymological sense, which we have last alluded to and which designates a thing that survives in itself, when it has lost its real point. Actually, the sole point of words is the expression of ideas; attributing a value to the words by themselves, independently of the ideas, failing even to base these words on any idea at all, and letting oneself be influenced by their mere sonority, is indeed superstition. 'Nominalism', in its different degrees, is the philosophical expression of this negation of the idea, for which it professes to substitute the word or the image; and in confusing conception and sensible representation, it really leaves nothing but the latter. In one form or another 'nominalism' is extremely rife in modern philosophy, while formerly it was no more than an exception. This is very significant; and it must be added that nominalism almost always goes hand in hand with empiricism, that is to say with the tendency to make experience, and especially experience of the senses, the origin and end of all knowledge. This negation of everything truly intellectual is what we always come back to, as common element, at the bottom of all these tendencies and all these opinions, because it is, in fact, the root of all mental deformation, and because this negation is implied, as the necessary starting-point, in all that contributes to pervert modern Western conceptions.

So far we have been mainly concerned with giving a general view of the present state of the Western world considered with regard to its mentality; this must come first, for it is on this that all the rest depends, and there can be no important and lasting change that does not start by influencing the general mentality. Those who maintain the contrary are still the victims of a very modern illusion. Seeing only the outward manifestations, they take the effects for the causes, and they readily believe that what they do not see does not exist. What is called 'historical materialism', or the tendency to trace everything to economic facts, is a remarkable example of this illusion. Things have reached such a state that the facts of this order have actually acquired, in the history of today, an importance which they never had in the past; but nonetheless the part they play is not and never can be exclusive. Besides, let there be no mistake about it: those 'in control', known or unknown, are well aware that, to act effectively, they must first of all create and keep up currents of ideas or of pseudo-ideas, and they do not fail to do so; even when these currents are purely negative, they are nonetheless of a mental nature, and it is in the minds of men that first the germs must be spawned that will later attain to outward realization; even for intellectuality to be done away with, minds must first be persuaded of its non-existence and their activity turned in another direction. This does not mean that we are among those who hold that the world is led by ideas directly; this again is a formula that has been much misused, and most of its users scarcely know what an idea is, even supposing that they do not confuse it altogether with the mere word. In other words, they are very often nothing more than 'ideologists', and the worst 'moralist' dreamers belong precisely to this category: in the name of the chimeras which they call 'right' and 'justice', and which have nothing to do with true ideas, they have had too fatal and lamentable an influence on recent events, an influence whose consequences are making themselves too keenly felt for it to be necessary to insist on what we mean. But the simpletons are not the only ones concerned: there are also, as always, those who lead them without their knowing it, who exploit them and make use of them in view of much more positive interests. In any case, as we are continually tempted to repeat, what matters above all is to know how to put everything in its proper place; the pure idea has no immediate relation with the domain of action, and it cannot have the direct influence on outward things that sentiment has; but the idea is, nonetheless, the principle, the necessary starting-point of all things, without which they would be robbed of any sound basis. Sentiment, if it is not guided and controlled by the idea, brings forth nothing but error, disorder, and obscurity; there is no question of doing away with sentiment but of keeping it within its legitimate bounds, and the same applies to all the other contingencies. The restoration of a real intellectuality, even if at first it was only within a limited elite, appears to be the sole means of putting an end to the mental confusion that reigns in the West. It is only this which could disperse the mob of empty illusions that encumber modern minds, and of superstitions far more ridiculous and unfounded than all those which are made a butt for random mockery by people who seek to be thought 'enlightened'; and it is only that which will make it possible to find a common ground for understanding with the peoples of the East. In fact, all we have said represents faithfully, not merely our own view—which in itself hardly matters—but also, what is far more worth considering, the judgment that is passed by the East upon the West, when Easterners deign to extend their interest in the West beyond merely counteracting its invasive action by that altogether passive resistance of theirs which the West cannot understand, because it implies an inner power of which it has no equivalent, and against which no brutal force can prevail. This power is beyond life, it is superior to action and to all that takes place, it has nothing to do with time, and partakes of supreme immutability; if the Easterner can patiently undergo the material domination of the West, it is because he knows how relative transitory things are, and because he carries, in the very depth of his being, the consciousness of eternity.

4

IMAGINARY TERRORS
AND REAL DANGERS

DESPITE THE HIGH OPINION which Westerners have of themselves and of their civilization, they are well aware that their control over the rest of the world is far from being definitely assured, and that it may be at the mercy of events that it is not within their power to foresee, still less to prevent. What they do refuse to see, however, is that the chief cause of the dangers that threaten them lies in the very character of the European civilization. Nothing that relies merely, as their civilization does, on the material order of things can hope for more than transitory success. Change, which is the law in this essentially unstable domain, may have the worst consequences in every respect, and these consequences will come with all the more lightning rapidity as the speed of change grows greater and greater, the very excess of material progress bringing with it the grave risk of ending in some cataclysm. One has only to think of the ceaseless perfecting of the means of destruction, of the increasingly important part that they play in modern warfare, of the scarcely reassuring prospects that certain inventions open up for the future, and one will hardly be disposed to deny such a possibility. Furthermore, the machines that are expressly intended for killing are not the only dangerous ones. Starting from the point that things have now reached, it does not need much imagination to picture the West ending by self-destruction, either in a gigantic war compared with which the last one will seem negligible, or through the unforeseen effects of some product which, when unskillfully manipulated, would be capable of blowing up, not merely a factory or a town as hitherto, but a whole continent. Certainly, it may still be hoped that

Europe and even America will pull themselves together and regain their self-control before reaching such extremities; lesser catastrophes may serve as useful warnings for them and, by the fear which they inspire, do something to arrest this dizzy course which can only lead to an abyss. All this is possible, especially if the fear is coupled with some overly strong sentimental disappointments such as may work upon the mass of the people to wipe out the illusion of 'moral progress'. Thus the excessive development of sentimentality might also contribute to this salutary result, and indeed it will have to, if the West, left to itself, is to look no further than in her own mentality for the means of a reaction which will become necessary sooner or later. Such means, however, would be far from sufficient to force upon Western civilization a change of trend, even if this reaction were to take place at once; and, as equilibrium is scarcely to be realized in such conditions, there would still be good reason to dread a return to barbarism pure and simple, as a quite natural consequence of the negation of intellectuality.

Setting aside for the moment these indications of a future which may be far off, it is clear that the Westerners of today are still apt to believe that progress, or what they call progress, can and must be unbroken and indefinite. While deluding themselves more than ever about their own importance, they have become the self-appointed missionaries for the world-wide propagation of this progress, imposing it, if need be, by force on those peoples who commit the offence—which is unpardonable in their eyes—of not eagerly accepting it. This rage for propaganda, which we have already alluded to, is very dangerous for everyone, but above all for the Westerners themselves, who make themselves dreaded and loathed as a result; the mania for conquest has never been developed so far, and until now there was never any question of hiding behind masks of hypocrisy such as belong to modern 'moralism'. The West forgets, moreover, that it had no historical existence at a time when the Eastern civilizations had already reached their full development;[1]

---

1. It is possible that there were earlier Western civilizations, but the present one is not their heir, and even the memory of them is lost, so that we need not concern ourselves with them here.

with its pretensions, the West seems to Easterners as a child might seem if, proud at having hurriedly acquired some scraps of rudimentary information, it should believe itself to possess the sum of all knowledge and should wish to teach it to old men full of wisdom and experience. This mistake would be harmless enough, and no more than amusing, if Westerners had not brutal force at their disposal; but the use that they make of it entirely alters the situation, since it is there, and not in an 'assimilation', that the true danger lies for those who, quite without wanting to, come into contact with them. Indeed, Westerners are quite incapable of assimilating others to themselves, being qualified neither intellectually nor even physically; European peoples, no doubt because they are made up of heterogeneous elements and do not strictly speaking constitute one race, are those whose racial characteristics are the least firmly fixed and the first to disappear when there is a mingling with other races; wherever such mixtures occur, it is always the Westerner who, far from being able to absorb the others, is absorbed himself. As for the intellectual point of view, the considerations that we have just been putting forward make it needless for us to insist on it; a civilization that never ceases to move, that has neither tradition nor deep-rooted principle, obviously cannot have a real influence on those which possess those very things that it lacks itself; and if the inverse influence is in fact no longer exerted, it is simply because Westerners are incapable of understanding what is strange to them: they are impervious, in this respect, merely through mental inferiority, whereas the Easterners are so out of pure intellectuality.

There are truths which it is necessary to emphasize again and again, however unpalatable many people may find them. All the superiorities on which Westerners preen themselves are purely imaginary, with the sole exception of material superiority. This one is only too real; and no one denies it them, while, at heart, no one envies them for it either; but the trouble is that they abuse it. For anyone who has the courage to see things as they are, colonial conquest cannot, any more than any other armed conquest, base itself on any other right than that of brute force. By all means let it be said that a people that feels itself too cramped at home must enlarge its field of activity, and that it can only do so at the expense of those who are too weak to resist it. We do not even see how things of this kind could be prevented from happening, but at least let there be no pretence of acting in the interests of 'civilization', which are quite beside the point. That is what we call 'moralist' hypocrisy: it is unconscious in the masses of the people, who never fail to accept with docility whatever ideas are inculcated, but it ought not to be equally so with everyone, and we cannot admit that statesmen, in particular, are the dupes of the phraseology which they use. When a European nation seizes some country, even if it should be only inhabited by truly barbarian tribes, no one will convince us that it is for the pleasure or the honor of 'civilizing' these poor people, who have shown not the least desire for it, that a costly expedition is undertaken, followed by all sorts of public works. A man must be very ingenuous indeed if he can help realizing that the true motive is quite different, and that it lies in the hope of more tangible profits. The chief object, whatever pretexts are put forward, is to exploit the country, and very often, if possible, its inhabitants at the same time, for they could not possibly be suffered to go on living there in their own way, even if they are untroublesome. But since the word 'exploit' sounds bad, one speaks, in the modern idiom, of 'developing the resources' of a country: it is the same thing, but a change of word is all that is needed to save the sensibility of the public from being shocked. Naturally, when the conquest has been carried out, the Europeans give free rein to their proselytism, because for them it is a real need. Each people brings to the task its own particular temperament, some performing it more brutally, others with more moderation, and the latter attitude, even when it is not calculated, is without doubt the more clever of the two. As for the results obtained, it is always forgotten that the civilization of certain peoples was not made for others of different mentalities. In the case of savages, the harm is perhaps not very great, and yet, in adopting the outward features of the European civilization (for their assimilation of it remains very superficial), they are generally more prone to imitate its evils than to take what good it may have. We have no desire to insist on this aspect of the question, which we are only considering incidentally; what is more serious is that the Europeans, when they find themselves face to face with civilized peoples, treat them like savages, and it is then that they make themselves really intolerable; and we are not speaking only of the rather dubious people from among whom colonists and officials are too often drawn, but of the Europeans almost without exception. The minds of men, especially of those who never cease to talk about 'right' and 'liberty', must be in a strange state when they are so prone to deny civilizations other than theirs the right to an independent existence; that is all that is asked of them in many cases, and it is not asking too much. There are some Easterners who, on this sole condition, would even agree to a foreign administration, so little do they care about material contingencies; it is only when it attacks their traditional institutions that they begin to find European domination intolerable. But it is just this traditional outlook that Westerners are more hostile to than to anything else, because they are all the more afraid of it the less they understand it, being themselves without it; such men are instinctively afraid of everything that goes beyond them; all their attempts in this respect will always go on being in vain, for there is a force there whose immensity they do not suspect; but if their indiscretion brings certain mishaps upon them, they have only themselves to blame. Furthermore, in the name of what, it may be asked, do they seek to force everyone to interest themselves exclusively in what interests them, to put economic concerns above all, or to adopt the political regime which they happen to prefer, and which, even admitting it to be the best for certain peoples, is not necessarily so for all? And the most extraordinary thing is that they have similar pretensions not only with regard to the peoples that they have conquered, but also with regard to those among whom they have succeeded in introducing and installing themselves while seeming to respect their independence; in fact, they extend these pretensions to the whole of mankind.

If this were not so, there would not be, in general, prejudices or systematic hostility against Westerners; their relations with other men would be what the relations between different peoples normally are; they would be taken for what they are, with the qualities and faults that belong to them, and, in spite of a possible regret that no truly interesting intellectual relations could be kept up with them, there would be scarcely any attempt to change them, for the

Easterners are not in the least given to proselytizing. Even those of the Easterners who seem to be most closed to everything foreign, the Chinese for example, would not be repelled by the sight of Europeans coming individually to set up house among them for business purposes, if they did not know only too well, from sad experience, what they are exposing themselves to by letting them have their way, and what encroachments quickly follow on what seemed, in the beginning, to be so inoffensive. The Chinese are the most deeply pacific people that exists; we say pacific and not 'pacifist', for they feel not the least need to build up grandiloquent humanitarian theories on that score: their temperament makes war repellent to them, and that is all. If this is a weakness in a certain relative sense, there is, in the very nature of the Chinese race, a force of another order which makes up for it, and the consciousness of which undoubtedly goes toward making this peaceful frame of mind possible. This race is gifted with such a power of absorption that it has assimilated all its successive conquerors, and done so with incredible rapidity, as history shows. Nothing, therefore, could be more ridiculous than the imaginary terror of the 'yellow peril' invented one day by William II, who even symbolized it in one of those so-called 'mystical' pictures which he liked to fill up his spare time by painting. No one, without all the ignorance that most Westerners suffer from, and their incapacity to see how much the rest of mankind differs from themselves, could possibly imagine the Chinese rising up in arms and marching forth to conquer Europe;[2] a Chinese invasion, if it should ever take place, could only be a peaceful penetration, and that is not, in any case, a very imminent danger. It is true that if the Chinese had the Western mentality, the hateful imbecilities that they are publicly credited with on every occasion would have been quite enough incitement for them to send out expeditions into Europe; much less would serve the West as a pretext for armed intervention, but these things leave the Easterners altogether indifferent. No one

---

2. Whereas the march of events in China since the first publication of this book might seem to contradict this assertion, it should be recalled that it was 'revolutionary' China, and hence precisely a 'China' that had turned against its own tradition, that became aggressive. ED.

has ever, to our knowledge, dared to tell the truth about the origin of the events which took place in 1900. Here it is in a few words: the precincts of the European legations in Peking were not subject to the jurisdiction of the Chinese authorities, and a veritable den of robbers had been formed in the out-buildings of the German legation by people who were under the patronage of the Lutheran mission; these people used to spread themselves through the town, pillage as much as they could, and then, with their spoils, retreat into their refuge where, as no one had the right to pursue them, they were sure of impunity; in the end the townspeople were exasperated and threatened to invade the legation precincts so as to take hold of the malefactors who were there; the German minister wished to stop this and set himself to harangue the mob, but he only succeeded in getting killed in the turmoil; to avenge this outrage, an expedition was organized at once, and the strangest thing is that all the European states, even England, let themselves be drawn in the wake of Germany; the spectre of the 'yellow peril' had at least served some purpose in this case. It goes without saying that the belligerents got considerable benefits out of their intervention, especially from an economic point of view; and the profits made out of the mishap were not even confined to states as a whole: we know individuals who were placed in most fortunate circumstances in recognition of their military service... in the cellars of the legations; there would be no need to go and tell these people that the 'yellow peril' is not a reality!

It may, however, be objected that not only are there the Chinese, but also the Japanese, and that these latter are certainly a warlike people; that is true, but in the first place the Japanese, who come from a mixture in which Malayan elements predominate, do not really belong to the yellow race, and consequently their tradition is bound to be of a different character. If Japan is today ambitious to have the hegemony of the whole of Asia and to 'organize' it after its own fashion, it is precisely because Shintoism, a tradition in many ways very unlike Chinese Taoism, and one which gives much prominence to ritual warfare, came into contact with nationalism, learnt of course from the West—for the Japanese have always been only too clever at imitation—and has been changed into an imperialism very like what is to be found in certain other countries. However, if the Japanese attempt such an undertaking, they will meet with at least as much resistance as the Europeans do, and perhaps even more. In fact, the Chinese evince for no one such hatred as for the Japanese, no doubt because the Japanese, as their neighbors, seem to them particularly dangerous; they dread them as a man who loves his quiet dreads everything that shows signs of disturbing it, and above all they despise them. It is only in Japan that the so-called 'progress' of the West is eagerly received, and this eagerness is all the greater because they think they can make 'progress' serve toward their realizing this ambition that we have just spoken of; and yet superiority in armaments, even combined with the most remarkable fighting qualities, does not always prevail against certain forces of another order: this was brought home to the Japanese in Formosa, and they do not find Korea an altogether untroublesome possession either. In fact, if the Japanese very easily won a war that a large part of the Chinese knew nothing of until it was over, it is because they were for the moment favored, for special reasons, by certain elements that were hostile to the Manchu dynasty, and that knew very well that other influences would intervene in time to prevent things from going too far. In a country like China, many events, such as wars or revolutions, take on quite a different aspect according to whether they are looked at from far or near, and, however surprising it may seem, it is distance that enlarges them: seen from Europe, they look considerable; in China herself, they dwindle down to mere local incidents.

It is by an optical illusion of the same kind that Westerners give undue importance to the movements of turbulent small minorities, formed of people who are often quite unheard of by their own compatriots, and who, in any case, are totally ignored by them. We are referring to a few individuals, such as are to be found more or less in all Eastern countries today, who have been brought up and educated in Europe or America, and who, having lost through this education the sense of tradition and knowing nothing of their own civilization, think it as well to affect the most extreme 'modernism'. These 'young' Easterners, as they call themselves to make their tendencies more marked, could never acquire a real influence in the East;

sometimes, like puppets, unknown to themselves, they are used for playing a part that they have no idea of, being manipulated with all the greater ease because they take themselves very seriously; but it also happens sometimes that after renewing contact with their race they are gradually disabused, realize that their presumption was chiefly the result of ignorance, and end by becoming true Easterners once more. These elements are merely exceptions of the very lowest order, but, as they make a certain amount of noise which carries into other countries, they attract the attention of Westerners, who naturally look on them with sympathy, and who, in doing so, lose sight of the silent multitudes compared with which these few are quite inexistent. The true Easterners scarcely trouble about making themselves known to foreigners, and this accounts for some rather strange errors: we have often been struck by the ease with which people come to accept, as authentic representatives of Eastern thought, one or two incompetent and unauthorized writers, sometimes even in the pay of a European power, and almost exclusively putting forward ideas that are entirely Western. Because they have oriental names, they are taken eagerly at their word, and henceforth, since there are no means of judging them by comparison, all their fellow countrymen are credited with conceptions or opinions which only belong to these few, and which are often poles apart from the Eastern outlook; of course, their output is strictly reserved for the European or American public, and in the East no one has ever heard of them.

Apart from the individual exceptions just spoken of, and also the collective exception of Japan, material progress really interests no one in these Eastern countries, where it is held to have brought few advantages and many disadvantages; but there are, with regard to it, two different attitudes, which outwardly may even seem conflicting, though they proceed nonetheless from one and the same standpoint. There are some who will not hear this so-called progress spoken of at any price and, retiring into a shell of purely passive resistance, go on behaving as if it did not exist; the others, looking on this progress as an unpleasant necessity, imposed by circumstances that will not last, prefer to accept it for the time being, simply and solely because they see, in the instruments which it puts at their disposal, a means of resisting Western domination more effectively and of hastening its end. These two currents run throughout the East, in China, in India, and in the Islamic countries. If the present tendency may seem to be for the latter to prevail over the former, it would be very rash to draw the conclusion that there has been any deep change in the East's way of existence; the whole difference amounts to no more than a mere question of timeliness, and it is not on such a basis that there could be a real renewal of relations with the West, but quite the contrary. Though some Easterners seek to promote in their country an industrial development which would enable them, for the future, to struggle without being at a disadvantage against the peoples of Europe—meeting them on the very ground over which these peoples extend their whole activity—they nonetheless, we maintain, give up nothing of what is the essence of their civilization. Besides, economic rivalry can only be a new source of conflicts, unless an understanding is reached in another domain and from a higher point of view. There are, however, some Easterners, very few, who have come to the following conclusion: since Westerners are definitely unamenable to intellectuality, let there be no longer any question of it; but, even so, friendly relations might perhaps be established in a purely economic way with some peoples of the West. That also is an illusion: either there must be agreement in the domain of the principles to start with, and then all the secondary difficulties will be smoothed away automatically, or else no real agreement of any sort will ever be reached; and it is for the West to take, if it can, the first steps toward an effective renewal of intellectual relations, since it is the misunderstanding hitherto shown by it that has actually given rise to all the obstacles.

It would be as well if Westerners would become resigned to seeing the cause of the most dangerous misunderstandings where it really lies, that is, in themselves, and rid themselves of these ridiculous terrors of which the all too familiar 'yellow peril' is certainly the extreme example. The spectre, too, of 'Pan-Islamism' has a way of being conjured up, regardless of facts: in this case there is no doubt that the fear is less absolutely devoid of foundation, for the Islamic peoples, occupying the place of intermediaries between the East and the West, combine certain characteristics of both, and they are, for example, much more warlike than the pure Easterners; but when all is said and done there is no need to exaggerate. True Pan-Islamism is primarily a statement of principle, essentially doctrinal in character; for it to take the form of political vindication, the Europeans would have to have compromised themselves considerably; in any case, it has nothing in common with any sort of 'nationalism', which is quite incompatible with the fundamental conceptions of Islam. The fact is that in most cases (and here we are thinking chiefly of North Africa) a clearly understood policy of 'association', respecting Islamic legislation in its entirety and implying a definite renunciation of all attempt at 'assimilation', would probably be enough to do away with the danger, if danger there be. Considering, for example, that the conditions imposed for obtaining French naturalization amount quite simply to an abjuration of the Islamic faith (and there are many other facts that might be mentioned in the same connection), it is small wonder that there are frequent jars and difficulties that might easily be avoided by a truer understanding of the situation. But, once again, it is precisely this understanding which the Europeans lack altogether. What must not be forgotten is that the Islamic civilization, in all its essential elements, is strictly traditional, as are all the Eastern civilizations; this is quite a sufficient reason to prevent Pan-Islamism, whatever form it may take, from ever identifying itself with Bolshevism or other such movements, as one or two misinformed people seem to fear. We have not the least desire to give here an account of Russian Bolshevism, for it is very difficult, as far as this is concerned, to know exactly what to go on; no doubt the reality is rather different from what it is generally reputed to be, and more complex than its opponents and champions think; but it is at least certain that the movement is clearly anti-traditional and therefore altogether modern and Western in outlook. It is utterly absurd to claim that the German or even the Russian mentality is in opposition to the outlook of the West, and we do not know what sense words can have for those who maintain such an opinion, any more than for those who describe Bolshevism as 'Asiatic'; in fact, Germany is on the contrary one of the countries where the Western outlook is carried to its extreme pitch; and, as for the Russians, even if they have derived some outward characteristics from the Easterners, they are also as far removed from them intellectually as it is possible to be. We should add that when we speak of the West, we also include Judaism, which has never exerted any influence except in a Westerly direction, and which may even have helped somewhat toward forming the modern mentality in general. In point of fact, the large part played in Bolshevism by Israelite elements is a serious reason for the Easterners, and for the Muslims above all, to be distrustful and to keep their distance; we are not speaking of certain agitators of the 'Young Turk' type, who are profoundly anti-Muslim, being not seldom also of Jewish origin, and not having the least authority. Bolshevism cannot penetrate into India either, because it is opposed to all the traditional institutions, and especially to that of the castes; from this point of view, the Hindus would see no difference between its destructive action and the destructive action that the English have long tried to carry out by every sort of means, and where the one has failed, the other would be no more successful. As for China, she is generally very much out of sympathy with everything Russian, and moreover the traditional outlook is no less firmly established there than in all the rest of the East; if certain things can be tolerated more easily there for the moment, it is because of this power of absorption that is inherent in the Chinese race, and that enables it to turn in the end to its own advantage even a momentary disorder. In fact it would be quite irrelevant, for the sake of bringing credit to the legend of non-existent and impossible agreements, to mention the presence in Russia of a few bands of mercenaries who are no more than common brigands, and whom the Chinese are very glad to be rid of at their neighbors' expense. When the Bolsheviks tell of champions gained for their ideas among the Easterners, it is either mere boasting or self-deception. The truth is that some Easterners see in Russia, Bolshevist or no, a possible means of help against the domination of certain other Western powers, but they have not the slightest interest in Bolshevist ideas, and furthermore, if they consider a temporary agreement or alliance as acceptable in certain circumstances, it is because they know perfectly well that these ideas can never take root in their country; otherwise they would beware of showing them the least semblance of favor. It is quite possible for a state to accept as auxiliaries, in view of a certain definite course of action, people with whom it has no common thought, and for whom it feels neither respect nor sympathy; for the true Easterners, Bolshevism, like everything else which comes from the West, will never be anything but a brutal force. If this force can do them some passing service, they will undoubtedly be glad of it, but one may rest assured that, as soon as there is nothing more to be got from it, they will take all the necessary steps to prevent it from becoming harmful to them. Besides, the Easterners, whose ambition it is to escape from the domination of one Western power, would certainly never consent to place themselves, for the sake of realizing this ambition, in a situation that might involve their falling again immediately under the domination of another Western power; they would gain nothing by the change, and, as their temperament is opposed to all feverish haste, they will always prefer to wait for more favorable circumstances, however remote they may seem, rather than to expose themselves to such a risk.

This last remark may explain why those Easterners who seem most impatient to shake off England's yoke did not dream of taking advantage of the war in 1914 for this purpose: it was because they knew well that Germany, in case of victory, would not fail to impose on them at least a more or less disguised protectorate, and this further state of subjection was to be avoided at any price. No Easterner who has had a reasonably close view of the Germans thinks it possible to arrive at mutual understanding with them any more than with the English; the same applies to the Russians, but Germany, with her formidable organization, generally inspires, and with good reason, more fears than Russia. Easterners will never be for any European power, but they will always be against those, whichever they may be, that seek to oppress them, and against those only; as for the rest, their attitude can only be neutral. We are speaking, of course, from the political point of view alone and as far as states or collectivities are concerned; there may always be individual sympathies or antipathies which remain outside these considerations, just as, when we speak of Western lack of understanding, we have in mind only the general mentality, and not the possible exceptions. These exceptions, moreover, are very rare; nonetheless, if one is convinced, as we are, of the desirability of restoring proper relations between East and West, a beginning must certainly be made now to encourage this by all available means, however inadequate they may be; and the foremost of these means is to bring home, to those who are capable of understanding, what are the indispensable conditions of this restoration.

These conditions, as we have already said, are above all intellectual, and they are at the same time both negative and positive: firstly, all the prejudices, each of which is an obstacle, must be destroyed, and it is this end that is aimed at essentially by all the considerations which we have put forward so far; then there must be a restoration of true intellectuality, which the West has lost, and which the study of Eastern thought, if undertaken as it ought to be, can greatly help it to recover. In short, the Western outlook must be completely reformed; that is, at least, the ultimate goal to be reached; but this reform, at the beginning, could evidently not be realized except within a limited elite, though no more would be needed for it to bear fruit sooner or later, owing to the influence that this elite would not fail to exert, even without expressly seeking to do so, upon the whole Western world. This would be, in all probability, the sole means of rescuing the West from very real dangers which, though they are not those that it believes in, will become more and more imminent if it continues to go along its present path; and it would also be the sole means of saving, when the time came, all that might be worth keeping of Western civilization, that is, everything in it that may be in some ways advantageous and compatible with a normal state of intelligence, instead of letting the whole of it disappear in one of those cataclysms whose possibility we indicated at the beginning of the present chapter, without however wishing to venture upon the least prediction. Furthermore, in such an eventuality, an elite, if it was already intellectual in the true sense of the word, would alone be able to prevent a return to barbarism; and also, if this elite had had time to act deeply enough upon the general mentality, it would save the West from having to be absorbed or assimilated by other civilizations, a possibility which is much less terrible than the last, but which would give rise to some disadvantages, for a time at least, by reason of the ethnic revolutions which would have to lead up to this assimilation. At this point, before going any further, we are anxious to make our attitude quite clear: we are not attacking the West in itself, but only, which is quite different, the modern outlook, in which we see the cause of the West's intellectual ruin; nothing would be more desirable, in our opinion, than the reconstitution of a truly Western civilization on normal foundations, for the diversity of the civilizations, which has always existed, is the natural outcome of the mental differences that characterize the races. But diversity in the forms does not in the least exclude agreement on the principles; concord and harmony do not mean uniformity, and to think that they do would be to defer to those theories of utopian equality which are one of the very things we denounce. A normal civilization, in the sense in which we understand it, will always be able to develop itself without being a danger to other civilizations; being conscious of the exact place that it ought to occupy among mankind as a whole, it will know how to keep to it and will not create any antagonism, because it will not have any pretension toward taking the lead, and because it will abstain from all proselytizing. We would not venture to maintain, however, that a purely Western civilization would be quite the equal intellectually of the Eastern civilizations; the West of old, going back as far as history will let us, does not show itself to be fully their equal (except perhaps in certain very secret schools, which, for this reason, it is difficult to speak of with certainty); but there are nonetheless, in this respect, some things which are far from negligible, and which our contemporaries are quite wrong in systematically ignoring. Besides, if the West comes one day to hold intellectual relations with the East, we see no reason why it should not take advantage of them for supplying itself with what it may still lack; lessons or inspirations may be taken from others without giving up one's independence, especially if, instead of resting content with borrowings pure and simple, one knows how to adapt what has been acquired so that it may conform as well as possible with one's own mentality. But, once again, these are remote possibilities; and, while waiting for the

West to return to its own traditions, there is perhaps no other means of preparing for this return and recovering what is essential to it than to go by analogy with the traditional forms that still exist today, and that, as such, can be studied directly. In this way the West, through understanding the Eastern civilizations, would come nearer to being brought back into the traditional paths which it so rashly and foolishly broke away from, while, on the other hand, the return to this tradition would bring about of itself an effective re-establishment of relations with the East. These are two things which are intimately bound up with one another, from whatever angle they are looked at, and in our eyes they seem equally desirable, not to say necessary. All this will be made clearer by what we have yet to say; but it should already be clear that we are not criticizing the West for the empty pleasure of criticism, nor even for the sake of showing up her intellectual inferiority when compared with the East. If the work which is to be done first seems chiefly negative, it is because, as we said at the beginning, the ground must necessarily be cleared before it can be built on. In fact, if the West were to give up its prejudices, the task would be already half done, and perhaps even more than half, for nothing would stand any longer in the way of constituting an intellectual elite, and those with the faculties required for taking part in it, no longer seeing almost insuperable barriers set up before them by present conditions, would easily find from then on the means of using and developing these faculties, instead of having them cramped and stifled by the mental formation or rather deformation which is at present imposed on whoever has not the courage to place himself resolutely outside the ranks of convention. Besides, to take in the full inanity of the prejudices in question, there must already be a certain degree of positive understanding, and, for some at least, it is perhaps harder to reach this degree than to go further once it has been reached. For a well constituted intelligence, the truth, however high, should be more easily assimilated than all the idle subtleties that the 'profane wisdom' of the Western world delights in.

HOW THE DIFFERENCES
MIGHT BE BRIDGED

1

FRUITLESS ATTEMPTS

In considering the idea of a renewal of intellectual relations between the East and the West, we have not the slightest pretension of putting forward an idea that is new, which, moreover, is in no way necessary to make it interesting; the love of novelty, which is nothing else but the need for change, and the cultivation of originality, resulting from an intellectual individualism that borders on anarchy, are characteristics that belong exclusively to the modern mentality, being the outward signs of its anti-traditional tendencies. In fact, this idea of renewal may already have occurred to many people in the West, which does not rob it of any of its value or importance. But we must face the fact that so far it has had no result, and that the opposition has even grown more and more marked, which was the inevitable consequence of the West's going along her divergent course. It is, indeed, the West alone that must be held responsible for this widening distance, since the East, in her essence, has never varied; and all the attempts which did not take this fact into consideration were bound to fail. The great fault of these attempts is that they were always carried out along lines that were the inverse of those that alone could have made for success: it is for the West to approach the East, since it is the West that has gone astray, and her efforts to persuade the East to do the approaching will be in vain, for the East does not feel that it has any better reasons for changing today than it had during the last centuries. Of course, there has never been any question, for the Easterners, of excluding those adaptations which are compatible with the traditional outlook, but if someone comes and suggests a change that amounts to a subversion of the whole established order, they can only meet this suggestion with a flat refusal; and the spectacle offered them by the West is very far from being an eloquent reason why they should let themselves be persuaded. Even if the Easterners feel bound to accept material progress to a certain extent, their doing so will never amount to a radical change, because, as we have already said, they will not be interested in it; they will undergo it simply as a necessity, and they will find nothing in it except an additional motive for resentment against those who have obliged them to submit to it. Far from giving up what is for them the whole point of their existence, they will keep it more rigidly locked within themselves than ever, and they will make themselves more remote and more inaccessible.

Besides, as the Western civilization is by far the youngest of all, the rules of the most elementary politeness, if accepted as valid in relations between peoples or races as they are between individuals, should be enough to show the West that it is for her, and not for the others who are her elders, to take the first steps. True, it is indeed the West that went to seek out the Easterners, but with quite contrary intentions: it was not to learn from them, as behoves youths in the presence of old men, but to strive, by brutal or insidious means, to convert them to their own way of thinking, and to preach to them all sorts of things which are pointless so far as they are concerned, or which they have no desire to hear about. The Easterners, who have all a great regard for politeness, are shocked at this unseasonable proselytism as at something grossly vulgar; coming, as it does, to make itself felt in their own country, it amounts even to what is still more serious in their eyes, a breach of the laws of hospitality; and Eastern politeness, let it be well understood, is no vain formalism such as the keeping of the entirely outward customs to which Westerners give the same name: it has, underlying it, far deeper reasons, since it reflects the whole of a traditional civilization, whereas, in the West, these reasons having disappeared with the tradition, what remains is strictly speaking no more than superstition, quite apart from the innovations simply due to 'fashion' and to its unjustifiable whims, which amount to mere parody. But, to revert to proselytism, it is nothing for the Easterners, apart from all question of politeness, but a proof of ignorance and incomprehension, a token of the absence of intellectuality, because it essentially implies and presupposes sentimentality: propaganda can only be made for an idea if there is attached to it some sentimental interest, to the detriment of its purity; as for pure ideas, all that can be done is to expound them for those who are capable of understanding them, without the least anxiety to carry the convictions of anyone whatever. This unfavorable judgment, which proselytism calls down upon itself, is confirmed by everything that Westerners say and do; all those facts which they believe to be proofs of their superiority are for the Easterners just so many marks of inferiority.

Anyone who takes up an attitude outside all prejudice must indeed resign himself to admitting that the West has nothing to teach the East, except in the purely material domain, in which the East, we repeat, can find no interest, having at her disposal things besides which material considerations scarcely count, things which she is not disposed to sacrifice in return for vain and futile contingencies. Besides, industrial and economic development, as we have already said, can only provoke rivalry and strife between peoples; thus it could not possibly provide a ground upon which close relations might be re-established, unless it be maintained that at least one way of bringing them together is to make them fight against each other; but that is not how we understand it, and indeed it would be nothing but a very poor play on words. For us, when we speak of a re-establishment of close relations, it means agreement and not rivalry; besides, the sole purpose for which certain Easterners will tolerate economic development in their country, as we have explained, admits of no hope on this score. It is not the conveniences added by mechanical inventions to the outward relations between peoples which will ever give them the means of better mutual understanding; such conveniences can only bring about, in every field of activity, more frequent jars and wider conflicts; as for the agreements based on purely commercial interests, one should know only too well how high they are to be rated. Matter is, by its nature, a principle of division and separation; nothing that comes from it could possibly serve as a basis for a real and lasting union, and moreover, in the realm of matter, it is ceaseless change which is law. We do not mean that there should be no attention paid at all to economic interests; but, as we repeat again and again, one must know how to put each thing in its place, and the place that normally belongs to such interests is rather the last than the first. This is not to say, either, that they should make way for sentimental utopias in the form of a 'League of Nations'; such concerns are still less stable if that be possible, not even being founded on that gross and brutish reality which at least cannot be denied to things of the purely sensible order; and sentiment, in itself, is no less variable and inconstant than what belongs to the strictly material domain. Moreover, humanitarianism, with all its dreams, is very often nothing but a mask to cloak material interests, a mask that is imposed by 'moralist' hypocrisy. We are not inclined to believe in the disinterestedness of the apostles of 'civilization', and furthermore, if the truth be told, disinterestedness is not a political virtue. In fact, it is neither in economics nor in politics that the means of an agreement could ever be found, and it is only after the event and as a minor consideration that economic and political activity will be invited to share the benefits of this agreement; these means, if they exist, do not spring from the realm of matter nor from that of sentiment, but from a far deeper and firmer realm, which can only be that of intelligence. Only, we mean here intelligence in its true and complete sense; we are not referring to those counterfeits of intellectuality which the West unfortunately persists in presenting to the East, and which are, moreover, all that she can present, knowing no other and, even for her own use, having nothing else at her disposal; what is enough to satisfy the West in this respect is entirely unfitted to give the East the slightest intellectual satisfaction since it lacks everything that is essential.

Western science, even when not purely and simply confused with industry, even when considered apart from all practical applications, is still, in the eyes of the Easterners, nothing but this 'ignorant knowledge' that we have spoken of, because it is not attached to any principle of a higher order. Since it is limited to the sensible world, which it takes for its sole object, it has not, properly speaking, a speculative value of itself; even so, if it were a preparatory means for attaining to a knowledge of a higher order, the Easterners would be much inclined to respect it, though they would think this means a very roundabout one, noticing especially how little it was adapted to their own mentality; but it is not such a means. This science, on the contrary, is fated, by its very constitution, to produce a state of mind that culminates in the denial of all other knowledge, and that we have named 'scientism'. Either it is taken for an end in itself, or else its only results are in the realm of practical applications, that is, in the lowest order of all, where the very word 'knowledge', with the fullness of meaning which the Easterners attach to it, can no longer be used except by the most illegitimate of extensions. The theoretic results of analytical science, however considerable they may seem to Westerners, loom only very small in the eyes of the Easterners, on whom it all makes the impression of childish pastimes, unworthy to retain for long the attention of those who are capable of applying their intelligence to other objects, or, in other words, of those who possess true intelligence, for everything else is only a more or less dim reflection of it. So much for the 'high idea' which the Easterners, according to Westerners (Leibnitz, for example, whom we have already mentioned in this connection), may come to have of European science. The same applies even if they are presented with its most authentic and complete products, and not merely with the rudiments of 'popularization'; it is not that they are incapable of understanding and appreciating it, but on the contrary because they rate it at its true value, with the help of a term of comparison which Westerners lack. European science, in fact, because there is no depth to it, and because it is really nothing more than it seems, is easily accessible to anyone who will take the trouble to study it. Every science, no doubt, is specially fitted to the mentality of the people that produced it, but in this particular case there is not the least equivalent of the difficulties encountered by those Westerners who wish to penetrate the 'traditional sciences' of the East, difficulties which arise from the fact that these sciences spring from principles that these would-be students have no idea of, and that they use means of investigation which are wholly foreign to the West, because they go beyond the narrow bounds that limit its outlook. The lack of adaptation, if it exists on both sides, takes very different forms: for the Westerners who study Eastern science, it shows itself as an almost irremediable failure to understand, however much they apply themselves to the task, and though individual exceptions are always possible, in this case they are very rare; for the Easterners who study Western science, it is simply a question of lack of interest, which is no bar to understanding, but which naturally makes them little inclined to devote to this study energies that might be better employed. Thus there must be no counting on scientific propaganda, nor on any other kind of propaganda either, for the bringing together of East and West; the very importance that Westerners attach to these methods and sciences gives the Easterners a poor enough opinion of their mentality, and, if they consider such things intellectual, it is because intellectuality has not the same meaning for them as for the Easterners.

All that we say about Western science can be said also about philosophy, and the plight of the latter is still more serious in that, while its speculative value is neither greater nor more real, it has not even that practical value which, however relative and secondary it may be, is still nonetheless something; and from this point of view we can couple with philosophy everything which, in science itself, has only a purely hypothetical character. Besides, in modern thought there can be no deep gulf between scientific and philosophic knowledge; the former has come to embrace everything which this thought has access to, and the latter, so far as it remains valid, is no more than a portion or mode of it, which is only given a place apart as a result of habit, and for reasons that are on the whole more historical than logical. If philosophy has the greater pretensions, so much the worse for it, since these pretensions can be founded on nothing; within the limits of the present state of the Western mentality, the only legitimate conception is the positivist one, which is the normal culmination of 'scientistic' rationalism, or else the pragmatist one, which definitely sets aside all speculation so as to keep to a utilitarian sentimentality: here we are face to face once again with these two tendencies between which the whole of modern civilization oscillates. For the Easterners, on the contrary, the alternative thus expressed has no meaning, because what really and essentially interests them is far beyond these two terms, just as their conceptions are beyond all the artificial problems of philosophy, and as their traditional doctrines are beyond all systems, those purely human inventions in the narrowest sense of the word human, invented, that is, by an individual reason, which, failing to understand its limitations, believes itself capable of embracing all the Universe or of reconstructing it at its fancy's whim, and which on 'principle'—to crown all—absolutely denies everything that goes beyond it. This amounts to denying metaphysical knowledge, which is supra-rational, and which is pure intellectual knowledge, knowledge at its highest. Modern philosophy cannot admit the existence of true metaphysics without destroying itself, and as for 'pseudo-metaphysics' which it incorporates, it is merely a more or less clever assemblage of exclusively rational hypotheses, which are therefore scientific in reality, and which are generally not based on anything very serious. In any case, the range of these hypotheses is always extremely limited; the few valid elements that may help to make up the mixture never go much further than the domain of ordinary science, and their close association with the most deplorable fantasies, no less than the systematic form given to the whole, can only invalidate them altogether in the eyes of the East. Easterners have not that special manner of thought which is generally known as philosophy: it is not among them that the systematic spirit and intellectual individualism are to be met with; but, if they have not the disadvantages of philosophy, they have, unadulterated by any alloy, the equivalent of all that may be interesting in it, which, in their 'traditional sciences', even takes on a much higher significance; and they have, besides this, immeasurably more, since they have, as principle of all the rest, metaphysical knowledge, whose domain is absolutely unlimited. That is why philosophy, with its attempts at explanation, its arbitrary demarcations, its useless subtleties, its ceaseless confusions, its aimless discussions, and its inconsistent verbiage, seems to them like a particularly puerile game; we have mentioned elsewhere the appreciation of the Hindu who, on hearing expounded for the first time the conceptions of certain European philosophers, declared that the ideas in them would only do credit, at the most, to a child of eight. Thus philosophy is still less to be counted on than ordinary science for inspiring the Easterners with admiration, or even for impressing them favorably, and it should not be imagined that they will ever adopt these ways of thinking, whose absence in a civilization is nothing to be sorry for, and whose characteristic narrowness is one of intelligence's greatest dangers; for the Easterners, as we were saying, it is all no more than a mere counterfeit of intellectuality, for the exclusive use of those who, through incapacity to see higher and further, are condemned, by their own mental constitution or by the effects of their education, to be forever ignorant of what true intellectuality is.

We have still a little more to say as regards in particular the 'philosophies of action': these theories really do nothing but sanction the complete overthrow of intelligence. Perhaps it is better in one sense to give up frankly all appearance of intellectuality than to go on deluding oneself indefinitely with mock speculations, but then why persist in wanting to evolve theories any longer? To claim that action must be put above all, through the incapacity to reach pure speculation, is an attitude which is really a little too like that of the fox in the fable… However that may be, there can be no self-delusion about converting Easterners to such doctrines, for whom speculation is incomparably superior to action; moreover, the taste for outward action and research after material progress go closely together, and there would be no need to revert to the question if our contemporaries did not feel that they must 'philosophize' on this subject, which shows clearly that philosophy, as they understand it, may in reality be anything but true wisdom and pure intellectual knowledge. Since this opportunity presents itself, we will take advantage of it to dispel at once a possible misunderstanding: to say that speculation is superior to action is not the same as saying that everyone ought equally to cease all interest in the latter; in a human society organized hierarchically each one must have assigned to him the function that suits his own individual nature, and that is the principle which essentially underlies, in India, the institution of the castes. If, then, the West ever comes again to have a hierarchic and traditional constitution, that is, a constitution founded on true principles, we do not in the least maintain that the Western masses will become as a result exclusively contemplative, nor even that they will have any obligation to be so to the degree that the Eastern masses are. Such a state might in fact be reached in the East, but there are, in the West, special conditions of climate and temperament which go against it and which always will. Intellectual aptitude will no doubt be much more widespread than it is today, but—what is still more important—speculation will be the normal occupation of the elite, and it will even be inconceivable that a true elite can be anything but intellectual. This alone, moreover, is enough to ensure a state of affairs that would be the entire opposite of what we see today, when material wealth almost totally replaces all genuine superiority, chiefly because it corresponds directly to the concerns and ambitions of the modern Westerner, with his outlook wholly confined to this earth, and secondly because it is the only kind of superiority (if indeed it can be called one at all) that the mediocrity of the democratic mind can adapt itself to. Such a reversal makes it possible to gauge the full extent of the transformation that must take place in the Western civilization for it to become normal again and comparable to other civilizations, and for it to cease being a cause of trouble and disorder in the world.

It is not unintentionally that we have so far refrained from mentioning religion among the different things which the West has to offer the East; it is because, though religion is also something Western, it is by no means modern, and, furthermore, it is a target for all the concentrated animosity of the modern mind, being the sole element in the West that has kept a traditional character. We are, of course, only speaking of religion in the proper sense of the word, and not of the deformations or imitations which, on the contrary, come to birth under the influence of the modern outlook, and which bear its mark so plainly that there is practically no difference between them and philosophical 'moralism'. As for religion proper, the Easterners can have nothing but respect for it, precisely because of its traditional character; furthermore, if Westerners were more attached to their religion than they usually are, they would certainly be much better thought of in the East. But an important point to remember is that tradition does not take on the specifically religious form among the Easterners, with the exception of the Muslims, and the Muslims, it must be remembered, have something of the West about them. Now the difference of outward forms is only a question of adaptation to the different mentalities, and where the tradition has not spontaneously taken the religious form, it is because it had definitely no need to do so. The error consists here in wanting to make the Easterners adopt forms that were not made for them, and that do not correspond to the requirements of their mentality, although they acknowledge how excellent such forms are for Westerners: that is why Hindus may be sometimes seen encouraging Europeans to return to Catholicism, and even helping them to understand it, without being in the least drawn to it on their own account. The traditional forms are no doubt not entirely equivalent, because they correspond to points of view which really differ; but, insofar as they are equivalent, the substitution of one for the other would be clearly useless; and, insofar as they are different otherwise than in expression (which does not in the least mean that they may be opposed or contradictory), this substitution could only be harmful, because it could only lead to faulty adaptation. If the Easterners have no religion in the Western sense of the word, they have as much of it as is fitted for them; at the same time, they have more from the intellectual point of view, since they have pure metaphysics, of which theology, all told, is merely a partial translation, tinged with the sentiment that is inherent in religious thought as such; if they have less on another side, it is only from the standpoint of sentiment, and because they can well do without it. What we have just said shows also why, in our eyes, the most satisfactory solution for the West is the return to its own tradition, with any gaps in the domain of pure intellectuality to be filled in as the occasion arises (which, moreover, only concerns the elite); religion cannot fill the place of metaphysics, but the two are not in the least incompatible, and the proof of this lies in the Islamic world, with the two complementary aspects of its traditional doctrine. Let us add that even if the West repudiates sentimentalism (and we mean by that the predominance of feeling over intelligence), the Western masses will retain nonetheless a need for satisfactions derived from sentiment, which the religious form alone can give them, just as they will retain a need for outward activity which the Easterners do not feel at all. Each race has its own temperament, and, though it is true that these are mere contingencies, it is, notwithstanding, only a fairly limited elite that can afford to disregard them. But, as for the satisfactions in question, it is in religion proper that Westerners in the normal course can and should find them, and not in those more or less extravagant makeshifts where men are preyed upon by the 'pseudo-mysticism' of some of our contemporaries, which is nothing more nor less than troubled and perverted religiosity, being yet another symptom of the mental anarchy which the modern world is suffering from, and which it may even die of, if effective remedies are not applied before it is too late.

Thus, among the manifestations of Western thought, some are simply ridiculous in the eyes of the Easterners, and these are all the ones that are specifically modern; the others are respectable, but they are exclusively suited to the West alone, although modern Westerners have a tendency to depreciate or reject them, no doubt because they are the surviving representatives of something too high for them. It is, then, quite out of the question, from whatever side one likes to look at it, that true relations should be re-established to the detriment of the Eastern mentality; as we have already said, it is for the West to approach the East; but for the approach to be effective, even good will would not be enough, and what is needed above all is understanding. So far those Westerners who have striven to understand the East, with more or less seriousness and sincerity, have only arrived in general at the most lamentable results, because they have brought into their studies all the prejudices that their minds were encumbered with, the more so because they were 'specialists', having inevitably acquired beforehand certain mental habits which they could not get rid of. To be sure, among the Europeans who have lived in direct contact with the Easterners, there are one or two who have been able to understand and assimilate certain things, just because, not being 'specialists', they were freer from preconceived ideas; but, as a rule, these people have not written; what they have learnt they have kept to themselves, and besides, the lack of understanding shown by any other Westerners whom they may have spoken to about it was well calculated to discourage them and lead them to be as reserved as the Easterners. The West, as a whole, has never been able to benefit from certain individual exceptions; and, as for the works that have been produced about the East and its doctrines, it would in most cases be better not to know of their existence, for ignorance pure and simple is far preferable to false ideas. We do not want to repeat all that we have already said elsewhere about the productions of the orientalists: their chief effect is, on the one hand, to mislead the Westerners who have recourse to them without having from other sources the means of correcting their mistakes, and, on the other hand, to give the Easterners, by the misunderstanding there displayed, the most unfavorable idea of Western intellectuality. In this latter respect, these productions merely confirm the opinion which everything else that the Easterners know of the West has already inclined them to hold, and accentuate their attitude of reserve that we were speaking of just now; but the former inconvenience is even more serious, especially if it is the West that must take the initiative in re-establishing intellectual relations. Actually, anyone who has a direct knowledge of the East can, when reading the worst translation or the most fantastic commentary, quite well extract the particles of truth that remain after all, unknown to the author who has merely transcribed without understanding, and who has only lighted on the correct word by a sort of fluke (this happens chiefly in the English translations, which are done conscientiously and without too much systematic bias, but also without any concern for true understanding); he can often even restore the meaning where it has been disfigured, and in any case he can consult works of this kind with impunity, even if he gains nothing from them; but for other people it is quite different. The ordinary reader, who has no means of checking their accuracy, can only take up one of two attitudes: either he honestly believes that the Eastern conceptions are in fact what they are made out to be, and feels a very understandable distaste for them—which serves meanwhile to strengthen all his Western prejudices—or else he realizes that these conceptions cannot, in actual fact, be so absurd or so devoid of sense, and feels more or less confusedly that there must be something else in them, but does not know what that something can be, and, in despair of ever knowing it, loses all interest in the matter, and will not even give it another thought. In this way, the final result is always a widening, and not a narrowing, of the gulf. We are only referring, of course, to people who are interested in ideas, for it is only among such that there is a possibility of finding those who might understand if given the means; as for the others, who merely look at it from the standpoint of curiosity and scholarship, we need not bother about them. Moreover, most orientalists are not and do not wish to be anything but scholars; so long as they confine themselves to historical or philological works it does not matter very much; it is clear that such works cannot serve in the least toward the end that we have in view, but their only real danger is the one which is common to all the abuses of scholarship, and which consists in the spread of the 'intellectual short-sightedness' that limits all knowledge to research after details, and the frittering away of efforts that might in many cases be better employed. But much more serious in our eyes is the influence exerted by those of the orientalists who profess to understand and to interpret the doctrines, and who make the most incredible travesty of them, while asserting sometimes that they understand them better than the Easterners themselves do (just as Leibnitz imagined that he had recovered the true meaning of the characters of Fu Hsi), and without ever dreaming of accepting the opinion of the authorized representatives of the civilizations that they seek to study. This should be the first thing for them to do; instead they act as if called upon to reconstruct vanished civilizations.

This incredible pretension merely betrays the Westerners' belief in their own superiority: even when they consent to take the ideas of others into consideration, they deem themselves so intelligent that they must needs understand these ideas much better than do the people who elaborated them: just a glance from the outside, and they know fully what to make of them; a man who has such confidence in himself generally lets slip all the opportunities that he might have of obtaining real instruction. Among the prejudices that go toward keeping up such a state of mind there is one that we have called the 'classical prejudice', and that we alluded to in connection with the belief in a single and absolute 'civilization', the prejudice being, in fact, nothing more than a particular form of this belief. Because the modern Western civilization considers itself the heir to the Greco-Roman civilization (which is only true up to a certain point), it is not thought desirable to know anything that lies beyond,[1] on the conviction that the remainder is not interesting or that it can only be the object of a sort of archaeological interest. The law is laid down that elsewhere there can be no valid ideas, or that at least, if one or two happen to occur, they must have existed also among the ancient Greeks and Romans. It is however something to be truly thankful for if this is all, and if they are not made out to be borrowings from classical sources. Even those who do not think expressly along these lines submit nonetheless to the influence of this prejudice: there are some who, while displaying a certain sympathy for Eastern conceptions, wish at all costs to make them fit into the frames of Western thought, which amounts to disfiguring them altogether, and which proves that in point of fact they understand nothing about them. Some, for example, will not see in the East anything but religion and philosophy, that is, just exactly what is not there, and as for what really is there they see nothing of it at all. No one has ever pushed these false assimilations further than have the German orientalists; it is precisely they whose pretensions are the greatest, and who have come to monopolize almost entirely the interpretation of the Eastern doctrines. With their narrowly systematic cast of mind, they have not merely made philosophy out of them, but something altogether like their own philosophy, whereas the things in question have nothing whatever to do with such conceptions. Evidently, they cannot resign themselves to not understanding, nor help reducing all things to the level of their own mentality, thinking the while to do great honor to those whom they are crediting with these ideas that would be 'good for children of eight.'

Besides, in Germany, the philosophers themselves have had a direct hand in this work, and Schopenhauer in particular must certainly take a large share of responsibility for the way in which the

---

1. In a speech delivered in the French Chamber of Deputies by M. Bracke, during a debate on educational reform, we noticed this very characteristic passage: 'We are living in the civilization of Greece and Rome. For us there is no other. The civilization of Greece and Rome is, for us, Civilization with a capital letter.' These words, and above all the unanimous applause that greeted them, fully justify all that we have said elsewhere about the 'classical prejudice'.

East is interpreted. And how many people, even outside Germany, go about repeating, after him and his disciple Hartmann, trite sentences on 'Buddhist pessimism', which they readily suppose to be the basis of the Hindu doctrines! There are also a good number of Europeans who are so ignorant as to imagine moreover that India is Buddhist, and, as always happens in such cases, they do not fail to talk at random. Furthermore, if the public attributes an undue importance to the deviated form of Buddhism that developed in India, the mistake is owing to the incredible number of orientalists who have specialized in it, and who have, moreover, found the means of deforming even this deviation of the Eastern outlook. The truth is that no Eastern conception is 'pessimistic', and that even Buddhism is not. It is true that there is no 'optimism' there either, but that proves simply that these labels and classifications do not apply, any more than do all those others which are likewise made for European philosophy, and that things do not appear in this light to the Easterners. To look at things in terms of 'optimism' or 'pessimism' requires Western sentimentality (this same mentality which led Schopenhauer to look for 'consolations' in the Upanishads), and the deep serenity that the Hindus find in pure intellectual contemplation lies far beyond those contingencies. We should never finish if we wished to bring to light all the mistakes of this kind, a single one of which is enough to prove total lack of understanding; our intention is not to give here a catalogue of the setbacks, German or otherwise, which the study of the East, undertaken on faulty foundations and apart from any true principle, has culminated in. We have only mentioned Schopenhauer because he is a very 'representative' example. Among the orientalists proper we have already referred above to Deussen interpreting India by means of this same Schopenhauer's conceptions; we will call attention also to Max Müller's endeavoring to discover 'the germs of Buddhism', that is, of heterodoxy, even in the Vedic texts themselves, which are the essential foundations of traditional Hindu orthodoxy. We could go on like this almost indefinitely, even while only noting one or two features in the work of each; but we will confine ourselves to adding one last example, because it shows up clearly an altogether characteristic bias; it is that of Oldenberg sweeping aside *a priori* all the texts that speak of doings which seem miraculous and asserting that they must merely be considered as later additions, not only in the name of 'historical criticism', but under the pretext that the 'Indo-Germans' (*sic*) do not admit miracles. Let him speak, if he will, in the name of the modern Germans, who are not for nothing the inventors of the so-called 'science of religions'; but that he should have the effrontery to associate the Hindus with his negations, which are those of the anti-traditional outlook, is something that passes all bounds. We have already said elsewhere what is to be thought of the hypothesis of 'Indo-Germanism', which scarcely exists but for political reasons: the Germans' orientalism, like their philosophy, has become an instrument in the service of their national ambition, which, however, does not mean that its representatives are necessarily dishonest; it is not easy to see what limits there are to the blindness that is caused by the intrusion of sentiment into domains that should be reserved for the intelligence. As for the anti-traditional outlook, which is at the bottom of 'historical criticism' and of all that is connected with it more or less directly, it is purely Western and, in the West itself, purely modern. No amount of insistence here can be too much, since it is this anti-traditionalism that is particularly repellent to the Easterners, who are essentially traditionalists and who, if they were not, would no longer be anything at all, since everything that makes up their civilizations is rigidly traditional. It is, then, this outlook which must be got rid of before anything else if there is to be any hope of an understanding with them.[2]

Apart from the more or less 'official' orientalists, who have at least in their favor, for want of other more intellectual qualities, an honesty that is generally indisputable, there is nothing, in the way of

---

2. For want of an opportunity to examine it closely enough, we cannot say much about the most recent of the pseudo-oriental attempts that have cropped up in Germany, that of Count Keyserling, who has founded a 'School of Wisdom' at Darmstadt; but it seems that its underlying conception is chiefly a 'philosophy of life', that is, yet another purely Western thing. Moreover, we have reasons for thinking that Count Keyserling has not been altogether unconnected with the Theosophist movement or its derivations; in any case the information that we have been able to get from Hindu sources with regard to him is altogether unfavorable.

Western presentations of the Eastern doctrines, but the daydreams and vagaries of the Theosophists, which are nothing but a tissue of gross errors, made still worse by methods of the lowest charlatanism. To this subject in particular we have already devoted an entire work,[3] where, in order to give all the pretensions of these people their full deserts and to show that they have no right to claim any credentials from the East, but quite the contrary, we have simply had to appeal to the most rigorously established historical facts; so we do not wish to go into the question again, but we could not help calling to notice here their existence at least, since one of their claims is precisely the establishment, after their fashion, of relations between East and West. There again, even apart from the political undercurrents that play a considerable part in these organizations, it is the anti-traditional outlook which, under cover of a pseudo-tradition born of pure fancy, gives itself free rein in these inconsistent theories whose woof is spun from an evolutionist conception; beneath the bits and pieces borrowed from the most varied traditions, and behind the Sanskrit terminology, which is used almost always in diametrically the wrong sense, there is nothing but purely Western ideas. If these could contain the elements of a mutual approach, then it would have to be brought about, all things considered, entirely at the expense of the East: concessions as far as mere words go would be made, but the East would be asked to give up all of its essential ideas, and also all the institutions that it is attached to. However, the Easterners, above all the Hindus who are aimed at more particularly, are far from being duped and know perfectly well what to make of the real tendencies of such a movement; one cannot expect to seduce them by offering them a gross caricature of their doctrines, even supposing that they had no other motives for being distrustful and keeping their distance. As for those Westerners who, even without being truly intelligent, have a certain amount of common sense, they pay little heed to these extravagances, but the unfortunate part of it is that they let themselves be too easily persuaded that such things are Eastern, when they are nothing of the

---

3. *Theosophy: History of a Pseudo-Religion*. See also the final chapter of *Introduction to the Study of the Hindu Doctrines*.

sort. Besides, even common sense is becoming strangely rare today in the West, and minds are becoming more and more unbalanced, which accounts for the present success of Theosophism and of all the other more or less analogous undertakings that we bring together under the general heading of 'Neo-Spiritualism'. While there is no trace of 'Eastern tradition' among the Theosophists, the occultists are equally lacking in authentic 'Western tradition'. Once again, there is nothing serious in any of it, but merely a confused and, on the whole, incoherent 'syncretism', in which the ancient conceptions are interpreted most falsely and quite arbitrarily, and which seems to be made simply to serve as a disguise for the most extreme modernism. If there are any 'archaisms' in it, they are merely in the outward forms, and both ancient and medieval Western conceptions meet with almost as total a lack of understanding there as the Eastern ones do in Theosophism. Certainly, it is not through occultism that the West will ever be able to recover its own tradition, any more than it will be able to rejoin Eastern intellectuality, and for the same reasons; here again, these two things are closely bound up one with another, whatever may be thought by certain people, who see oppositions and antagonisms where there cannot possibly be any. It is precisely the occultists who, some of them at any rate, believe themselves bound not to speak of the East, which they know absolutely nothing about, except with injurious epithets that betray a real hatred, and probably also spite caused by the feeling that the Easterners have knowledge which they will never succeed in penetrating. We are not reproaching either Theosophists or occultists with a lack of understanding which, after all, they are not responsible for; but let anyone who is Western (from the intellectual point of view, we mean) acknowledge it openly, and not put on an Eastern mask; let anyone who has the modern outlook at least have the courage to admit it (there are so many who glory in it), and not claim support from a tradition that is not his. In denouncing such pieces of hypocrisy we are of course only thinking of the leaders of the movements in question, not of their dupes; but it must be said that unconsciousness often goes with dishonesty, and that it may be difficult to determine exactly the part played by either—is not 'moralist' hypocrisy also as a rule unconscious? Moreover, it makes little difference to the results, which are all that we seek to guard against, and which this unconsciousness does not make any the less deplorable: the Western mentality becomes more and more warped in every way; it wanders and is scattered in all directions, a prey to a most obscure disquiet, haunted by the darkest nightmares of a delirious imagination. Is this really 'the beginning of the end' for modern civilization? We do not want to make any rash supposition, but at least there are many signs that should give food for reflection to those who are still capable of it. Will the West be able to regain control over herself in time?

Keeping to what can be stated as actual facts, and not anticipating the future, we will say this much: all the attempts that have been made so far to bring East and West together again have been undertaken in the interests of the Western outlook, and that is why they have failed. This is true, not only of all propaganda openly Western (and that is the form which these attempts usually take), but also just as much of the ventures that claim to be based on a study of the East: there is far less effort to understand the Eastern doctrines in themselves than there is to reduce them to the level of Western conceptions, which amounts to mutilating them altogether. Even where there is no conscious and avowed bias toward depreciating the East, it is nonetheless implicitly assumed that whatever the East possesses is possessed also by the West as a matter of course; now that is utterly untrue, especially with regard to the West of today. Thus, through an incapacity for understanding which is largely due to their prejudices (for, while there are some who are born with this incapacity, there are others who acquire it only under the influence of preconceived ideas), Westerners do not attain in the slightest degree to Eastern intellectuality. Even when they imagine that they grasp it and that they are translating the writ that expresses it, they are simply making a caricature, and, in the texts or in the symbols they believe themselves to be explaining, they merely fish out again what they have put there themselves, that is, Western ideas: the fact is that the letter is nothing by itself, and that the spirit escapes them. In these conditions, the West cannot get outside the limits that hedge her round, and since, within these limits beyond which nothing really exists for her any longer, she goes on and on ceaselessly and simultaneously exploring material and sentimental paths that lead her always further and further away from intellectuality, it is clear that she can only grow more and more markedly divergent from the East. We have just seen why even the orientalist and pseudo-oriental attempts contribute to this themselves. Once again, it is the West that must take the initiative, but she must really be prepared to go toward the East, not merely seeking to draw the East toward herself, as she has tried to do so far. There is no reason why the East should take this initiative, and there would still be none, even if the Western world were not in such a state as to make any effort in this direction useless; but on the other hand, if a serious and fully conscious attempt were made starting from the West, the authorized representatives of all the Eastern civilizations could not fail to receive it very favorably. This chapter has taken into consideration what we had already said in the first part of the book, and it now remains for us to show how the West might attempt to approach the East. We have shown that it is specifically Western mental tendencies that make impossible all intellectual relations between the two; and without first reaching some mutual understanding on this intellectual ground, all else will be quite in vain.

2

AGREEMENT ON PRINCIPLES

When wishing to talk about principles to our contemporaries, it does not do to hope that they will be made to understand easily, for most of them have not the slightest idea what these things can possibly be, and in fact do not even suspect that they may exist; to be sure, they also talk about principles, and they even talk too much about them, but not once without applying this word to whatever least fits its meaning. Thus, in our epoch, the name 'principles' is given to scientific laws a little more general than the rest, whereas they are really just the opposite, being conclusions and the results of induction, even when they are not mere hypotheses. Thus—and this is still commoner—the same name is given to moral conceptions, which are not even ideas, but the expression of one or two sentimental aspirations, or to political theories, often equally based on sentiment, such as the all too familiar 'principle of nationalities', which has contributed to the disorder of Europe more than one can possibly imagine. Do not some people even go so far as to speak unhesitatingly of 'revolutionary principles', as if it were not a contradiction in terms? The misuse of a word to such an extent means that its true significance has been completely forgotten; this case is altogether like that of the word 'tradition', applied, as we were saying just now, to no matter what purely outward custom, however banal and insignificant it may be; and, to take yet another example, if Westerners had kept the religious sense of their ancestors, would they not avoid using on every occasion such phrases as 'religion of patriotism', 'religion of science', 'religion of duty', and others of the same kind? These are not pieces of linguistic slovenliness without greater import, but symptoms of the confusion that infests every part of the world: people can no longer distinguish between the most different standpoints and domains; they put one thing in the place of another that it has nothing to do with; and men's language, all things considered, merely gives a faithful representation of the state of their minds. As there is, moreover, a correspondence between mentality and institutions, the reasons for this confusion are also the reasons why it is thought that anyone, no matter who, can equally well fulfill any function, no matter what, the democratic slogan of equality being merely the consequence and the manifestation, in the social order, of intellectual anarchy. The Westerners of today are truly, in every respect, 'without caste', to use the Hindu expression, and even 'without family', in the sense that the Chinese give to the phrase; they have no longer anything of what constitutes the foundation and the essence of the other civilizations.

These considerations bring us precisely to our starting-point: modern civilization suffers from a lack of principles, and it suffers from it in every domain. By a monstrous anomaly, it is, alone among all the others, a civilization without principles, or with only negative ones, which amounts to the same thing. It is as if an organism with its head cut off went on living a life that was at the same time intense and disordered. The sociologists, who are so fond of likening collectivities to organisms (often quite unjustifiably) ought to reflect a little on this comparison. With the suppression of pure intellectuality, each special and contingent domain is looked on as independent; one infringes on the other, and everything is mingled and confused in an inextricable chaos. Natural relations are turned upside down and what should be subordinate proclaims itself autonomous mentally as well as socially, all hierarchy is done away with in the name of that hallucination, equality; and as equality is after all impossible in actual fact, false hierarchies are created, in which anything, no matter what, is given the highest rank, whether it be science, industry, morals, politics, or finance, for want of the one thing that can and must normally assume the supremacy, that is, once again, for want of true principles. Let people pause a little in the face of such a picture before crying out that it is an exaggeration; let them rather take the trouble to examine sincerely the state of things, and if they are not blinded by prejudice, they will realize that it is indeed as we described it to be. We do not in the least deny that there are degrees and stages in the disorder; it was not reached all in one stride, but it was inevitably fated that it should be reached, once given the absence of principles which, as it were, dominates the modern world and makes it what it is; and, at the point where we stand today, the results are already clear enough for some people to begin to be alarmed and to feel the threat of a final dissolution. There are some things that really cannot be defined except by negation: anarchy, in whatever realm it may be, is simply the negation of hierarchy, and it is nothing positive; all told, modern Western civilization is anarchic and unprincipled, and this is exactly the same thing that we express in other terms when we say that, unlike the Eastern civilizations, it is not a traditional civilization.

What we call a traditional civilization is one that is based on principles in the true sense of the word, that is, one where the intellectual realm dominates all the others, and where all things, science and social institutions alike, proceed from it directly or indirectly, being no more than contingent, secondary, and subordinate applications of purely intellectual truths. Thus a return to tradition and a return to principles are in reality just one and the same thing; but clearly the knowledge of the principles, where it is lost, must first be restored before there can be even a remote thought of applying them; it is quite out of the question to build up again a traditional civilization in all its fullness without first having the supreme and fundamental knowledge that must preside over the work. To seek to go about it otherwise would mean introducing still more confusion just where one hoped to abolish it, and it would also mean that one had failed to understand what tradition is in its essence; this is the case of all the inventors of pseudo-traditions of the kind we mentioned above; and if we insist on things that are so obvious, it is because the state of the modern mind compels us to do so, for we know only too well how hard it is to stop it from reversing the normal order of things.

The best intentioned people, if they are at all tainted with this mentality, even despite themselves and while declaring themselves its enemies, might be strongly tempted to begin at the end, but this would only be to give way, in their impatience to reach at once those visible and tangible results which are everything in people's eyes today, to that strange giddiness and love of speed that has overcome the whole West; indeed, modern minds have been turned so consistently toward outward things that they have become incapable of grasping anything else. That is why we repeat so often, at the risk of seeming tedious, that the necessary starting-point is the domain of pure intellectuality, and that nothing worthwhile will ever be done by starting from anywhere else. And everything connected with this domain, though not coming within the range of the senses, has consequences which are far more to be reckoned with than what depends on a contingent order of things. This is perhaps not easily taken in by those who are not used to the idea, but such is the case nonetheless. However, good care must be taken not to confuse the purely intellectual with the rational, the universal with the general, metaphysical knowledge with scientific knowledge; on this subject we will refer our readers to the explanations we have given elsewhere,[4] and we do not think that we need excuse ourselves for doing so, as there can be no question of reproducing indefinitely and unnecessarily the same considerations. When we speak absolutely of principles, without any specification, or of purely intellectual truths, it is always the universal order, and no other, that is in question; here lies the domain of metaphysical knowledge, that is, supra-individual and supra-rational knowledge itself, knowledge that is intuitive, beyond all analysis, and independent of what is relative. It should, moreover, be added that the intellectual intuition through which such knowledge is arrived at has absolutely nothing in common with these infra-rational intuitions, be they of a sentimental, instinctive, or purely sensible order, which are the only ones that come within the scope of present-day philosophy. Of course, the conception of metaphysical truths must be distinguished from their formulation, where discursive reason may intervene secondarily (on condition that it receives directly a reflection of pure and transcendent intellect) in order to express, as far as possible, these truths which lie far beyond its domain and its range,

---

4. *Introduction to the Study of the Hindu Doctrines.*

and of which, in view of their universality, no symbolic or verbal form can ever give anything but an incomplete, imperfect, and inadequate translation, such as is rather fitted to act as a support for the conception than to express effectively what is in itself, for the most part, inexpressible and incommunicable, and what cannot be 'experienced' except in a direct and personal way. Finally, let us mention once more that if we cling to this term 'metaphysics', it is solely because it is the most suitable of all those that the Western languages offer.

If philosophers have come to apply it to something quite different, the confusion is of their making, not of ours, since the sense in which we understand it is the only one that conforms to its etymological derivation, and this confusion, due to their total ignorance of true metaphysics, is quite analogous to those that we mentioned just now. We do not feel in the least bound to take these misuses of language into consideration, and it is enough simply to put people on their guard against the mistakes that might so arise. Since we take all due precautions in this respect, we see no serious disadvantage in using such a word, and we dislike having recourse to neologisms except where strictly necessary; moreover, such neologisms are a nuisance and might very often be avoided by taking care to fix, as clearly as need be, the meaning of the terms used, which would most certainly be better than inventing a wilfully complicated and involved terminology, after the fashion of the philosophers, who, it is true, get themselves in this way the cheap luxury of being thought original. If there are some people who dislike this term 'metaphysics', it may be added that the knowledge in question is knowledge in the highest sense of the word, knowledge unqualified, and the Hindus have, in point of fact, no other word to express it; but in the European languages we do not think that the use of this word would be likely to avoid all misunderstanding, since people have grown used to applying it, without qualifying it in the least, to science and philosophy. We shall, then, simply go on speaking of metaphysics as we have always done; but we hope that the explanations made necessary by our desire to be always as clear as possible will not be looked on as profitless digressions: they only seem to take us away from our intended subject, without actually doing so.

By reason of the very universality of the principles, it is there that the agreement should be most easily reached, and, furthermore, reached in an altogether immediate way: either a man succeeds in grasping them or he does not, but, having once done so, he cannot help but be in agreement. The truth is one and imposes itself alike on all those who know it, provided, of course, that they actually do know it with certainty; but an intuitive knowledge cannot be anything else but certain. In this domain one is outside and above all the particular points of view; the differences never lie in anything but the more or less outward forms, which are merely a secondary adaptation, and not in the principles themselves; it is the domain of what is essentially 'formless'. The knowledge of the principles is strictly the same for all those who possess it, for mental differences can only affect what belongs to the individual order and what is therefore contingent, and the domain of pure metaphysics does not come within their range; undoubtedly, each one will express in his own way what he has understood, as far as he can express it, but he who has truly understood will always be able, behind the diversity of the expressions, to recognize the one truth, and so this inevitable diversity will never be a cause of disagreement. However, this power to see through the many forms that serve more as a veil than as an expression of the truth implies that true intellectuality which has become so utterly foreign to the Western world; and in the light of this it is scarcely to be believed how futile and miserable all the philosophical discussions appear, bearing, as they do, on words far more than on ideas, even if the ideas are not wholly lacking. As for truths of a contingent order, the multiplicity of the individual points of view concerning them may give rise to real differences, which, moreover, are by no means necessarily contradictions; the fault of systematic minds lies in not acknowledging as legitimate any point of view but their own, and in condemning all that does not comply with it as wrong; but in any case, once given that the differences are real, even though they are reconcilable, agreement cannot be reached at once, especially as each one feels a natural difficulty in taking the others' standpoints, because his mental make-up does not lend itself to them without some revulsion. In the domain of principles there is nothing of the kind, and this explains the seeming paradox that what is highest in any tradition may be at the same time what is easiest to grasp and assimilate, apart from all considerations of race or epoch, and on the sole condition of having enough capacity for understanding; it is, in fact, what is freed from all contingencies. For all else in a tradition, on the contrary, and especially for everything that may be classed as 'traditional sciences', a special preparation is necessary, and as a rule it is rather a painful process for anyone not born in the civilization that has evolved these sciences; this is because mental differences intervene here, for the sole reason that the things in question are contingent, and the way that men of one race have of looking at these things, which is for them the most suitable way, is by no means equally suitable for men of other races. Within a given civilization, there may even be, in this order, adaptations that vary according to the different epochs, though they consist nonetheless in nothing but the strict development of the principles contained in the fundamental doctrine, which are thus made explicit to answer the needs of a particular moment, without its ever being possible to say that any new element has come to be added from outside. There cannot possibly be any real addition or change where an essentially traditional civilization is concerned, as is always the case in the East.

In the modern Western civilization, on the contrary, it is only the contingent things which people consider, and their way of doing so is truly chaotic because they lack the guidance that a purely intellectual doctrine alone can give, and that has no possible substitute. Obviously there is no question of contesting the results which are nonetheless arrived at in this way, nor of denying them any relative value; and it seems even natural that, within a given domain, the more narrowly a man limits his activity, the more results he will get from it. If the sciences which so interest Westerners had never previously reached anything like the development that these people have given them, it is because they used not to be thought important enough for such efforts to be devoted to them. But if the results are valid when each one is taken separately (which goes well with the entirely analytical character of modern science), the whole merely gives an impression of disorder and anarchy; no one bothers about the quality of the knowledge accumulated, but only about its quantity; the result is the scattering of energies amid an indefinite number of details. Furthermore, there is nothing above these analytical sciences: they depend on nothing and, intellectually, lead to nothing; the modern mind becomes more and more shrunkenly petty, and in this domain, which is really so minute though believed to be so immense, it confuses everything, drawing analogies between things that are quite unconnected, seeking to apply to one the methods that are exclusively suited to the other, transferring into one science the conditions which define a different one, and finally losing its way there, unable to find it again, for want of guiding principles. Thence springs the chaos of innumerable theories, of jarring, colliding, and conflicting hypotheses that overthrow and replace one another, until, with all hope of knowledge gone, it is even maintained that there is no point in searching except for searching's sake, that the truth is beyond man's reach, that perhaps it does not even exist, that there is no reason to worry about anything except what is useful or profitable, and that if, after all, one sees fit to call it true, there is no harm done. The intelligence that so denies the truth denies its own purpose, or, in other words, it denies itself. The ultimate outcome of Western science and philosophy is the suicide of intelligence; and perhaps this is, for some people, merely the prelude to that monstrous cosmic suicide dreamed of by certain pessimists who, failing to understand anything from their faint glimpses of the East, have mistaken for nothingness the supreme reality of metaphysical 'non-being', and for inertia the supreme immutability of the eternal 'non-action'!

The sole cause of all this disorder is ignorance of the principles; only let pure intellectual knowledge be restored, and all the rest will be able to grow normal again: it will then be possible to put all the domains in order once more, to set up what is definite and final in place of what is provisional, to wipe out all vain hypotheses, to throw the light of synthesis on the fragmentary results of analysis, and, by putting these results back into their place as part of a knowledge that is truly worthy of the name, to give them, although they must only rank as subordinates, an incomparably higher import than that which they can lay claim to at present. To do this, true metaphysics must first be sought out where it still exists, namely, in the East; and then, but only then, while retaining Western sciences insofar as they are valid and legitimate, it will be possible to think of giving them a traditional basis by linking them up once more with the principles in the way most suited to the objects of their research, and by giving them their rightful place in the hierarchy of knowledge. Wanting to start by establishing in the West something comparable to the 'traditional sciences' of the East amounts really to wanting the impossible; though it is true that the West also had once her 'traditional sciences', notably in the Middle Ages, it must be admitted that they are for the most part almost entirely lost, that even for what is left of them the key is missing, and that modern Westerners would find them just as impossible to assimilate as those used by the Easterners; ample proof lies in the painfully labored works of the occultists who have sought to take a hand in the reconstruction of such sciences. This does not mean that, after fulfilling the conditions indispensable for understanding, namely, after acquiring knowledge of the principles, there can be no inspiration taken from these ancient sciences at all, or from the Eastern ones either: both may no doubt be drawn on for certain elements that can be put to use, and above all they may serve as an example of what is to be done so as to build up other sciences analogous to them; but it will always be a question of adapting, and not of copying purely and simply. As we have already said, it is the principles alone that are strictly invariable; knowledge of them is the only knowledge that cannot be modified in any way, and moreover it contains in itself all that is necessary for bringing to birth, in all the relative orders, all the possible adaptations. That is why the secondary elaboration in question will be able to take place as it were of its own accord, as soon as this knowledge is there to preside; and if this knowledge is held by an elite that is powerful enough to put the community at large into the right frame of mind, all the rest will be brought about with seeming spontaneity, just as the fruits of the present frame of mind seem to be spontaneous; it is never more than mere seeming, for the masses are always influenced and guided unknown to themselves, but it is just as possible to guide them in a normal direction as it is to pervert them mentally and to keep them so perverted. The purely intellectual task, which must first of all be fulfilled, is then really the first in every respect, being at the same time the most necessary and the most important, since on it everything depends and from it everything is derived; but when we use this phrase 'metaphysical knowledge', there are very few indeed, among the Westerners of today, who have even the vaguest suspicion of all that it implies.

The Easterners (we are only speaking of those who really matter) will never take into account any civilization, unless, like theirs, it is traditional; but there can be no question of giving this traditional character overnight, without any preparation at all, to a civilization that is totally lacking in it; such dreams and utopias are not of our making, and it is better to leave to the unreflecting enthusiasts that incurable 'optimism' which makes them incapable of seeing what can or cannot be accomplished in given conditions such as these. The Easterners, who moreover attribute only a relative importance to time, know very well what it means, and they would never make any of the blunders that Westerners are liable to be drawn into by the unhealthy haste that brings all their undertakings to a fever pitch, whose stability is thus fatally undermined. No sooner do they think their purpose achieved than everything collapses; it is as if someone were to try building on a piece of shifting ground, without first taking the trouble to establish solid foundations, under the pretext that foundations cannot be seen. Certainly, those who might undertake a task like the one we are speaking of should not expect to obtain visible results immediately; but their work, far from being any the less real and effective, would on the contrary be the more so, and while having no hope of ever seeing it come outwardly to flower, they would reap many other satisfactions from it, gaining for themselves inestimable benefits. In fact, there is no common measure between the results of an altogether inward work of the highest order and all that can be obtained in the domain of contingency. If Westerners think otherwise, here too reversing the natural order of things, it is because they do not know how to rise above the world of the senses. It is always easy for a man to belittle what he has no knowledge of, and when he is incapable of reaching it, an assumed contempt is actually his best means of consoling himself for his impotence, and it is moreover a means that is at everyone's disposal. But it may be asked, if this is so, and if this inward work which must mark the beginning is in point of fact the sole truly essential one, why should one bother about anything else? The reason is that, although the contingencies are indeed no more than secondary, they nonetheless exist; seeing that we are in the world of manifestation, we cannot ignore them entirely; and besides, since everything is necessarily dependent on the principles, all the rest may be had, as it were, for the asking, and it would be a great mistake to shut one's eyes to this possibility. There is also another reason, more particularly concerned with the modern Western outlook: this outlook being what it is, there would be little chance of interesting even the possible elite (we mean those who have the necessary intellectual gifts, albeit undeveloped) in a realization that would have to remain purely inward, or that at any rate was only presented to it under this one aspect; it is far easier to arouse its interest by showing it that this realization must in fact lead, if only in the far future, to outward results; and this is, moreover, the strict truth. Though the end is always the same, there are many different ways of attaining it, or rather of approaching it, for as soon as the transcendent domain of metaphysics is reached all diversity vanishes.

Among all these ways, that particular one must be chosen which suits best the outlook of the people in question. Anything, or almost anything—especially at the beginning—may serve as a support and an opportunity; where there is no organized traditional teaching, it would sometimes be very hard, in the exceptional case of an intellectual development being brought about, to say what had been the moving factor, and the most different and most unexpected things may have served as its starting-point, according to the individual natures of those concerned, as well as to outward circumstances. In any case, being essentially devoted to pure intellectuality is no reason for losing sight of the influence that it can and must exert in every domain, no matter how indirectly, even if this influence does not proceed from an express intention. We will go on to add, although no doubt this may be rather more difficult to understand, that no tradition has ever forbidden those who, by its guidance, have reached certain heights to radiate downward to lower domains the spiritual influences which they have concentrated in themselves, nor, by so doing, are they liable to lose anything that they have acquired; indeed, such things cannot be taken away from them, and the influences will gradually distribute themselves throughout the different domains in hierarchy, and will spread there as a reflection of supreme intelligence and as a participation in it.[5]

Between knowledge of the principles and the reconstitution of the 'traditional sciences', there is another task, or another part of the same task, which could be fulfilled, one whose action would make itself more directly felt in the social order; it is moreover the only one for which the West might still, to a fairly large extent, find the means in herself, but this calls for some explanations. In the Middle Ages, Western civilization was undeniably traditional; the difficulty is to decide whether it was as completely traditional as the Eastern ones are, especially when it comes to bringing formal proofs one way or the other. To keep to what is generally known, the Western tradition, such as it was at that epoch, was a tradition which took the form of a religion; but that does not necessarily mean that there was nothing else there, or that a certain elite may not have attained to pure intellectuality, which is above all forms. We have already said that there is no incompatibility between the two, and we have quoted Islam as an example in this respect; if we mention it again here, it is because the Islamic civilization is just the one that comes in many ways nearest in type to the European civilization of the Middle Ages; there is an analogy there which it might be good to take into account.

Furthermore, it must not be forgotten that religious or theological truths, not being, as such, looked at from a purely intellectual point of view, and not having the universality that belongs exclusively to metaphysics alone, are only principles in a relative sense; if the principles proper, of which these are an application, had not been known by at least one or two persons fully conscious of their knowledge, no matter how few, we can hardly see how the tradition, outwardly religious, could have had all the influence which it did

---

5. This sentence contains a precise allusion to the Tibetan symbolism of *Avalokiteshvara*.

actually exert for so long a period, and have produced, in different domains which do not seem to concern it directly, all the results that history has chronicled and that its modern falsifiers cannot cover up entirely, try as they will. It must be admitted moreover that in the doctrine of the Scholastics there is at least a certain degree of real metaphysics, perhaps not free enough from philosophical contingencies, and not clearly enough distinguished from theology; to be sure, it is not metaphysics in the full sense, but, when all is said and done, it is metaphysics, while in modern philosophy there is no trace of it;[6] and the fact that there was metaphysics there means that this doctrine, as far as it goes, must necessarily be in agreement with every other metaphysical doctrine. The Eastern doctrines go much further, in many different ways, but there may have been in the Middle Ages of the West something to complement the outward teaching, and these complements, being exclusively at the disposal of very inaccessible bodies of men, may never have been formulated in any written text, so that there can only be found at the most, in this respect, symbolic allusions, clear enough for anyone who knows from other sources what is behind it all, but quite unintelligible to anyone else. We are well aware that there is at the moment, in many religious circles, a very definite tendency to deny all 'esoterism', for the past as well as for the present; but we believe that this tendency, besides possibly implying one or two concessions made involuntarily to the modern outlook, is largely due to people being a little too ready, whenever the word is mentioned, to think of the false esoterism of certain people today, which has absolutely nothing in common with the true esoterism that we have in mind, which has left many traces that can still be discovered by anyone who is free from all bias. But however that may be, there is one fact that is incontestable: medieval Europe had from time to time, if not continuously, relations with the Easterners, and these relations had considerable effect in the realm of ideas. It is known, but perhaps

---

6. Leibnitz alone tried to take up again certain elements borrowed from the Scholastics, but he mixed them with considerations of quite a different order, which rob them of almost all their significance, showing that he only understood them very imperfectly.

not fully as yet, how much medieval Europe owed to the Arabs, who are the natural intermediaries between the West and the more distant parts of the East; and there was also direct contact with central Asia and even with China. It would not be amiss to study, among other periods, that of Charlemagne and also that of the Crusades, for though they were times of outward strife, there were understandings too on a more inward plane, so to speak; and we must call attention to the fact that strife, roused in this case by the equally religious form of the two traditions in question, is quite pointless and cannot arise where a tradition not clothed in this form is in question, as is the case with the more Eastern civilizations; among these there can be neither antagonism nor even mere rivalry. But we shall have occasion later on to come back to this point; what we want to bring out for the moment is that the Western medieval civilization, with its truly speculative branches of knowledge (even without considering how far they went), and with its social constitution organized in hierarchy, had enough in common with the Eastern civilizations to admit (with the same reserve) of certain interchanges in the order of intellect, which the character of modern civilization, on the contrary, now makes impossible.

If some people, while admitting the absolute necessity for a regeneration of the West, are inclined to prefer a solution by which none other than purely Western means need be resorted to (and, in all conscience, nothing but sentimentality could so incline them), they will no doubt make this objection: why not return purely and simply, though with all the necessary social modifications, to the religious tradition of the Middle Ages? In other words, why not rest content, instead of looking further afield, with giving back to Catholicism once more the pre-eminence which it held at that time, with reconstituting, under an appropriate form, ancient 'Christendom', whose unity was broken by the Reformation and by the events that followed? To be sure, if that could be realized here and now, it would indeed be something achieved, and it would even go far toward clearing up the frightful disorder of the modern world, but unfortunately this is far from being so easy a task as it may seem to certain theorists, and all sorts of obstacles would soon be raised against those who were bent on any definite action along these lines. We need not enumerate all these difficulties, but we will point out that the mentality of the present day, taken as a whole, hardly seems liable to lend itself to a transformation of this kind, so that here too everything would have to be got ready from the very beginning, and this task, even if those willing to undertake it really had the means of doing so at their disposal, might be no less long and no less arduous than the one that we have in mind ourselves, and its results would be far more superficial. Besides, there is no proof that the traditional civilization of the Middle Ages had only an outward and properly speaking religious side; it is even certain that there was something else, if only scholastic philosophy, and we have just said why we think that there must have been still more, for this philosophy, despite its undeniable interest, remains always merely on the outside. Lastly, if the West were to hedge herself round like this with a special form, the understanding with the other civilizations could only be realized in quite a limited way, instead of first basing itself on what is most fundamental; and so, among the problems which concern it, many would still be left unsolved, not to mention that there would always be a cause for anxiety and a perpetual risk of ruining everything in the excess of Western proselytism, which cannot be definitely checked except by full understanding of the principles, and by the essential agreement which, without even having to be expressly formulated, would be the immediate result. However, it goes without saying that, if the work to be done in the two domains of metaphysics and religion could be carried out side by side, we should see no reason to be anything but thankful, as we are convinced that even if they both went on quite independently of one another, harmony would be the end-result. Besides, if the possibilities we have in mind are to come to anything, a strictly religious revival would be needed sooner or later in any case, religion being a form of tradition especially suited to the West: this revival may be a part of the work that awaits the intellectual elite, once it has been constituted, or else, if this work is already done beforehand, the elite will find there a fitting support for its own activity. The religious form contains everything that is needed by the vast majority of Westerners, who cannot really find in anything else the satisfactions that their temperament calls for; this majority will never need anything else, and it is with this form as vehicle that it will have to receive the influence of the highest principles, an influence which, although so indirect, will be nonetheless a real participation.[7] In this way there may be, in a full tradition, two complementary and superposed aspects, which cannot possibly contradict one another or come into conflict because they refer to two domains that are essentially distinct; the purely intellectual one, moreover, concerns directly none but the elite, which alone need necessarily be aware of the communication kept up between the two domains to ensure the perfect unity of the traditional doctrine.

In short, we should not like to be in the least exclusive, and we do not think that any work is useless, provided that it be directed along the right lines; efforts that merely concern the most secondary domains may also yield something that is not altogether negligible, with consequences which, though not to be put to an immediate application, may come into their own later and, fitting in with all the rest, play their part, however modest it may be, in the constitution of this whole which we have in mind for a future that is no doubt very far off. This is why there would be, from our point of view, nothing against a study of 'traditional sciences', whatever tradition they may belong to, in the case of someone wanting to undertake it without delay (not in their entirety, which for the moment is impossible, but at least in certain elements), provided firstly that the student has already enough information to keep him from losing his way, which in itself presupposes much more than one might think, and secondly that the study never causes him to lose sight of the essential. These two conditions, moreover, go closely together: he whose intellectuality is developed enough for him to devote himself with unerring confidence to such a study is no longer in danger of being tempted to sacrifice the superior to the inferior: in whatever domain he has to exert his activity, he will never see there anything but a piece of work that is auxiliary to what is achieved in the sphere of the principles. Under the same conditions, if in some of its conclusions 'scientific philosophy' happens

---

7. An analogy might well be drawn here with the caste system and its way of ensuring that everyone participates in the tradition.

accidentally to agree at times with the ancient 'traditional sciences', there may be some interest in calling attention to the fact, though at the same time care should be taken to avoid the slightest implication that the latter are on a level with any particular scientific or philosophic theory whatsoever, for all such theories change and pass away, whereas everything that has a traditional basis receives from that alone a permanent value which does not depend on the results of any subsequent research. Lastly, as regards points of contact or analogies, it is important never to let oneself be drawn into making false assimilations, seeing that one is dealing with modes of thought that are essentially different. It is impossible to be too cautious of saying anything that might be interpreted in this way, for most of our contemporaries, owing to the very narrowness of their mental horizon, are only too prone to see likenesses where there are none. Within these limits, we can say that everything done in a truly traditional spirit has a purpose, and a deep-seated purpose at that; but there is nonetheless a certain order to be observed, at least in a general way, according to the necessary hierarchy of the different domains. Furthermore, before anyone can have the full traditional outlook (instead of merely a 'traditionalist' one, which only implies a tendency or an aspiration), he must have already penetrated into the domain of the principles, at least enough to have received the inward guidance which, once found, can never be lost sight of.

3

CONSTITUTION OF THE ELITE AND THE PART TO BE PLAYED BY IT

WE HAVE ALREADY REFERRED several times in the foregoing chapters to what we call the intellectual elite. Our readers will no doubt have easily understood that what we mean by this has nothing in common with what, in the West of today, sometimes goes under the same name. Those scholars and philosophers who are held to be the greatest 'authorities' in their own special domains may be absolutely unqualified to belong to this elite; indeed, they very likely are so, owing to acquired mental habits and to the many prejudices that always go with them, and above all to that 'intellectual short-sightedness' which these habits most usually lead to. There may always be honorable exceptions, of course, but it would not do to count too much on them. Generally speaking, there is more good to be got out of an ignorant man than out of one who has specialized in an essentially limited branch of studies, and who has undergone the deformation which a certain kind of education brings with it. The ignorant man may have within him possibilities of understanding which he has merely not developed for want of an opportunity, and the more futile the method of administering education in the West, the more common such cases may be. The qualifications we have in mind when we speak of the elite cannot be gauged by any outward criterion, since they are purely intellectual, and the qualities that go to make them up have nothing to do with 'profane' teaching. There are people in some countries of the East who do not know how to read or write, yet attain to a very high rank among the intellectual elite. On the other hand it would be just as wrong to exaggerate one way as the other: because two things are independent, it does not follow that they are incompatible; and if, especially in the conditions of the modern Western world, 'profane' or outward teaching can provide one or two additional aids to action, it would assuredly be wrong to despise it unduly. But there are things which it is only safe to study after having already got that unerring inward guidance which we alluded to, and which ensures immunity against all mental deformation. Once this point has been reached, there is no longer any danger to fear, for the road always lies open ahead; any domain, no matter what, may be entered into without risk of losing the way or even of staying there overlong, for its exact importance is known in advance; it is no longer possible to be led astray by error in any shape or form, or to take it for truth, or to confuse the contingent with the absolute. To use the language of symbolism, we might say that one has both an infallible compass and an impenetrable suit of armor. But before getting so far, there is often a long period of striving to be gone through (we do not say always, as time is not an essential factor in this respect) and it is then that the very greatest precautions are necessary if all confusion is to be avoided, at least under present conditions, for clearly the same dangers cannot exist in a traditional civilization, where, moreover, those who are truly gifted in an intellectual way find everything made as easy as possible for them to develop their natural abilities: in the West, on the contrary, they cannot meet anything at the moment but obstacles, often insuperable ones, and it is only thanks to rather exceptional circumstances that it is possible to get out of the ruts of mental and social convention.

At present, then, the intellectual elite, according to our idea of it, simply does not exist in the West: the exceptions are too rare and too isolated to be looked on as constituting anything that might be so called, and, besides, they are on the whole really quite un-Western, since they consist of individuals who intellectually owe everything to the East, and who are thus almost in the same situation as the Easterners in Europe, knowing only too well what abyss separates them mentally from the men who surround them. Under these conditions one is certainly tempted to take refuge in silence rather than run the risk of being bruised against the wall of general indifference in an attempt to express certain ideas, or even of provoking hostile reactions; however, the conviction that certain changes are necessary brings with it the obligation to begin doing something toward them, and at least to give those who are capable of developing their latent faculties (for, after all, there must be some who are) the opportunity of doing so. The primary difficulty is to reach those who are so qualified and who may not have the least suspicion of their own possibilities; a subsequent difficulty would be to bring about a selection and to turn away those who might think themselves qualified without really being so, but it must be admitted that very likely this elimination would take place almost of itself. None of these questions arise where there is organized traditional teaching, which everyone may partake of according to his capacity and up to the very point that it is within his powers to reach; there are, in fact, means of deciding exactly the full extent of a given individual's intellectual possibilities; but that is a subject which is above all 'practical', if this word may be used in such a case, or, if it be thought better, 'technical', and there would be no point in treating of it with the Western world in its present state. Besides, we only want at the moment to make people aware in advance, rather remotely, of some of the difficulties that would have to be overcome for there to be the beginnings of organization, and for there to be the constitution, even in embryo, of an elite; it would be far too premature to try here and now to define the means of this constitution, as the means—assuming that it becomes one day possible to consider them—will necessarily depend to a great extent on circumstances, like everything which is properly speaking a question of adaptation. The only thing that can be accomplished for the moment is to give the possible elements of the future elite the consciousness, as it were, of themselves, and that can only be done by putting forward certain conceptions which, when they reach those who are capable of understanding them, will show them the existence of what they knew nothing about, and will at the same time make them see the possibility of going further. Everything related to the order of metaphysics has, in itself, the power of opening up boundless horizons to anyone who has a true conception of it. This is not a hyperbole or a figure of speech, but it must be understood quite literally, as an immediate outcome of the very universality of the principles. Those who simply hear talk of metaphysical studies, and of things that keep exclusively to the domain of pure intellectuality, can scarcely have any suspicion, at their first encounter, of all that this implies: the things in question are the most tremendous that exist, and compared with them everything else is mere child's play. Moreover, that is why those who seek to set foot in this domain without having the qualifications required for reaching at least the first stages of true understanding, withdraw of their own accord as soon as they find that they have incurred the liability of undertaking serious and real work; true mysteries defend themselves unaided against all profane curiosity, and their very nature protects them against all assaults of human folly, no less than against the powers of illusion that may be described as 'diabolical' (everyone being free to read into this word all the meanings that he pleases, literal, or figurative). For this reason it would be utterly childish to have recourse to interdictions which, applied in such an order of things, would be meaningless; such bans may be legitimate in other cases, which we do not intend to discuss, but they cannot concern pure intellectuality; and as to what goes beyond mere theory and calls for a certain reticence, those who have the right attitude need not be constrained in any way to ensure their always being as careful and discreet as is necessary; all this is far beyond the range of any outward formulas whatever, and has nothing to do with the more or less fantastic 'secrets' which are above all the plea of those who have nothing to say.

Since we have been led into speaking of the organization of the elite, we must go on to point out a mistake that we have often had occasion to notice: many people no sooner hear the word 'organization' than they imagine that there is something afoot which may be compared with the formation of a group or an association. That is utterly wrong, and those who conceive such ideas prove by so doing that they understand neither the sense nor the import of the question; the reasons for this should be already clear from what we have just been saying. True metaphysics cannot be enclosed in the formulas of a particular system or theory, and no more can the intellectual elite possibly put up with the forms of a 'society' founded with statutes, regulations, reunions, and all the other outward manifestations that this word necessarily implies—these things have nothing to do with true metaphysics. Even to begin with, so as to form as it were a first nucleus, such an organization could not help; it would be an extremely bad starting-point, and one that could scarcely lead to anything but a setback. In fact, not only is this form of 'society' useless in such a case, but it would be most dangerous, by reason of the deviations that could not fail to take place: however strict the selection was, it would be very difficult to prevent, especially at the beginning and among so ill-prepared a portion of mankind, the introduction of one or two individuals whose lack of understanding would be enough to compromise everything; and it is more than likely that such groups would run a very severe risk of letting themselves be led astray by the prospect of some immediate social action, perhaps even political in the narrowest sense of the word, which would be the most disastrous thing that could happen, and the one which would tell most against the end in view. There are only too many examples of such deviations: how many associations, which might have fulfilled a very high function (if not a purely intellectual one, at least bordering on intellectuality) by continuing along the lines that had been laid down for them at the outset, began almost at once to degenerate in this way! Some of them even went not only astray, but changed their course completely, though they still bear the marks of their original objective, and these remain very clear to the eye of anyone with knowledge to understand them. That is how there came about a total loss, after the sixteenth century, of what might have been saved of the heritage left by the Middle Ages; and we say nothing of the accompanying drawbacks, such as petty ambitions, personal rivalries, and other causes of dissensions which inevitably arise in groups that are so constituted, especially if account be taken, as it certainly must be, of Western individualism. All this shows clearly enough what should not be done; what should be done is perhaps less clear, and that is natural, since, at the point where we now are, no one can say exactly how the elite will be constituted, supposing that it ever should be; that is probably something that belongs to a distant future, and one should have no illusions in this respect. However that may be, we will say that in the East the most powerful organizations, those whose work is the most far-reaching, have absolutely nothing in common with 'societies' in the European sense of the word; sometimes, under their influence, more or less external societies are formed in view of some definite end, but these societies, being always temporary, disappear as soon as they have fulfilled the function allotted to them. The outer society, then, is in this case no more than an accidental manifestation of the already existing inner organization, and the latter, in all its essence, is always absolutely independent of the former; the elite does not have to take part in struggles which, whatever their importance, are necessarily outside its own domain; only indirectly can it play a social part, but this makes that part all the more effective, because, to be the true director of what is in motion, one must not be involved oneself in the movement.[1] Here, then, is just the inverse of the plan that would be followed by those who would want to begin by forming outward societies; these societies must merely be the effect, and not the cause; they could only be of use and there could only be a real point in them if the elite had already been brought into existence (in accordance with the saying of the Scholastics: 'to act, one must be'), and if it was strongly enough organized to be sure of preventing any deviation. It is only in the East that examples can now be found which would be suitable for drawing inspiration from: we have many reasons for thinking that the West also had, in the Middle Ages, some organizations of the same type, but it is at least doubtful whether sufficient traces have been left to make it possible to form an exact idea of them in any other way than by analogy with what exists in the East, this analogy being moreover founded, not on idle suppositions, but on signs which do not deceive if one already has a knowledge of certain things; furthermore, to know these things, search must be made where they are still to be found as part of a living present, for we are speaking, not of archaeological curiosities, but of knowledge that cannot be

---

1. Aristotle's 'unmoved mover' may be recalled here; naturally, this is susceptible of many applications.

anything but direct if it is to be of any use. This idea of organizations which do not take the form of 'societies' in any respect, which have none of the outward features that characterize such groups, and which for that reason are all the more sound because they are really based on what is immutable without allowing themselves to be adulterated with anything transitory, is an idea which is quite strange to the modern mentality, and we have had various opportunities of appreciating the difficulties that are to be met with by anyone who tries to make people understand it. Perhaps we shall find the means of coming back to it some day, as lengthy explanations on this subject would not come within the scope of the present work, where we merely allude to it incidentally so as to cut short any misunderstanding.

However, we do not mean to shut out any possibility, in this sphere any more than in any other, or to discourage any initiative, provided that it is capable of producing valid results without culminating in a mere waste of energy; we simply want to put people on their guard against false opinions and over-hasty conclusions. It goes without saying that if one or two individuals, instead of working by themselves, would rather meet together and form what one might call 'working groups', we should not see any danger in that by itself, nor even any inconvenience, provided that those who take part are fully aware that they have not the slightest need to resort to this outward formalism which looms so large in the eyes of most of our contemporaries, for the very reason that outward things are everything for them. Moreover, great care would have to be taken even in forming these groups, if any serious work was to be done in them and followed out to any lengths, and many precautions would be necessary, since everything accomplished in this domain brings into play powers that the ordinary man has no inkling of, and those who are indiscreet may find themselves at the mercy of strange reactions, at least so long as a certain level of understanding has not been reached. Besides, the questions of method, in this connection, are closely dependent on the principles themselves; it follows that they are much more important than in any other domain, and that they have consequences much more serious here than in the field of science, though even there they are far from being negligible. This, however, is not the place to dwell on all these considerations; we exaggerate nothing, but, as we have said right from the beginning, we do not want to cloak the difficulties either; adaptation to certain definite conditions is always extremely delicate, and without unshakable and very extensive theoretic information there can be no question of trying to realize effectively the least thing. Even to acquire this information is not such a light task for Westerners; in any case, and we can never be too insistent on it, this task is the necessary starting-point, and the one indispensable preparation, without which nothing can be done, and which all the ultimate realizations in any order of things essentially depend on.

There is still another point that calls for our explanation: we have said elsewhere that the Easterners would not fail to help the intellectual elite in the fulfilment of its task, as, actually, they will always be well disposed toward a re-establishment of relations which ought normally to exist: but that presupposes an already constituted Western elite, and for its actual constitution it is the West that must take the initiative. As things are now, the authorized representatives of the Eastern traditions cannot have any intellectual interest in the West: at least, they can only be interested in the rare individuals who approach them, directly or indirectly, and who are simply too much of an exception for there to be any possibility of considering general action. We can state the following definitely: never, so long as the conditions are not altogether changed, will any Eastern organization be able to have relations with any Western organization whatsoever, since it could only do so with an elite constituted in accordance with the true principles. Until that day, then, the Easterners can be asked for nothing more than inspiration, which is already a great deal, and this inspiration can only be transmitted by individual influences acting as intermediaries, not by any direct action on the part of organizations which, except in case of unforeseen upheavals, will never do anything to incur responsibility in the affairs of the Western world, and that is understandable, for these affairs, after all, do not concern them; Westerners are alone in being over-ready to meddle with other peoples' business. If no one in the West gives proof of both the will and the capacity to understand all that is necessary for entering into relations with the East, the Easterners will take good care not to intervene, knowing moreover that it would be useless; and, even if the West should be heading straight for a cataclysm, they can do no more than leave it to fend for itself. Indeed, how could anyone exert an influence on the West, even supposing that they wanted to, without finding there the slightest foothold?

In any case, as we repeat once again, it is for the Westerners to take the first steps; naturally, the Western masses do not enter into the question, and there cannot even be any question of a large number of individuals, which might in many ways do more harm than good; to begin with, only a few are needed, on condition that they are capable of understanding truly and deeply everything concerned. There is also another point to remember: those who have assimilated, by direct contact, the intellectuality of the East must needs confine themselves to playing the part of intermediaries that we mentioned just now; they are, owing to this assimilation, too near the East to do more; they can suggest ideas, put forward conceptions, point out what ought to be done, but not form on their own initiative an organization, which, coming from them, would not be truly Western. If there were still some individuals in the West, even isolated ones, who had kept intact the legacy of the purely intellectual tradition that must have existed in the Middle Ages, everything would be greatly simplified; but it is for these individuals to make known their existence and to put forward their claims, and so long as they have not done so it is not for us to settle that question. Failing this, which is unfortunately rather improbable, it is only what we might call an indirect assimilation of the Eastern doctrines that could bring to birth the first elements of the future elite; we mean that the initiative would have to come from individuals who had developed themselves through their understanding of these doctrines, but without being too directly connected with the East, and on the contrary keeping in touch with everything valid that may still exist in the Western civilization, and especially with the traces of the traditional outlook that have managed to survive there despite the modern outlook, chiefly under the form of religion. This does not mean that those who, intellectually, have become altogether Eastern must necessarily lose touch with these things, the less so for the simple reason that they are essentially representatives of the traditional outlook; but their situation is too unusual not to impose a very great reserve on them, especially so long as they are not expressly appealed to for collaboration. They must hold themselves in wait, like the Easterners by birth, and all that they can do more than these Easterners is to expound their doctrines in a form more suited to the West, and to bring out the possibilities of agreement which their understanding of these doctrines will have revealed to them; once again, they must rest content with being intermediaries whose presence shows that all hope of mutual understanding is not irremediably lost.

We trust that these reflections will not be taken for anything other than what they are, and that conclusions will not be drawn from them which might well be most out of keeping with our thoughts; if too many points remain indefinite, it is because it is unavoidable, and because future circumstances alone will make it possible for light to be thrown on them little by little. In all that is not purely and strictly doctrinal, contingencies come necessarily to play a part, and from them may be drawn the secondary means of realizing all plans of adaptation; we say the secondary means, for the sole essential means, as must not be forgotten, belongs to the order of pure knowledge (that is, knowledge so far as it is simply theoretical, leading up to fully effective knowledge, for this last is not a means, but an end in itself, with regard to which any application is merely like an 'accident' which cannot possibly affect it or be a determining factor of it). If we take care, in such questions as these, to say neither too much nor too little, it is because, on the one hand, our intention is to make ourselves understood as clearly as possible, and because, on the other hand, we must nonetheless leave room for the possibilities, now unforeseen, which circumstances may bring to light later; the elements that might come into play are exceedingly complex, and, with things as unstable as they are in the Western world, it would be impossible to overestimate the importance of the part thus to be played by the unforeseen, which we do not say is absolutely unforeseeable, but which we do not admit the right to anticipate. That is why all that can be said with precision is mostly negative, in the sense that it is in answer to objections, some being actually formulated while others are only considered as possible, or in the sense that it clears away mistakes and misunderstandings and different forms of incomprehension, so far as they happen to meet the eye; but by such a process of elimination the question comes to be set in a much clearer light, which, all told, is already an appreciable result and, however things may seem, a truly positive one. We are well aware that Western impatience does not take at all easily to such methods, and that it would be more inclined to sacrifice certainty in the interests of speed; but it is not for us to make any concession to the demands of this impatience, which allow nothing firm to be set up, and which are altogether opposed to the end that we have in view. Those who are not even capable of restraining their impatience would be still less able to carry out the least work of a metaphysical order: let them simply try, as a preliminary exercise that does not commit them to anything, to concentrate their attention on one single idea, no matter what, for half a minute (it does not seem too much to ask), and they will see whether we are wrong to question their capabilities.[2]

And so we will add nothing further about the means by which an intellectual elite may come to be constituted in the West; even assuming that all goes in its favor, it does not look as if this constitution were anything like immediately possible, which does not mean that now is not the time to begin thinking about how things may be made ready for it. As for the part that will devolve on this elite, it follows clearly enough from all that has so far been said: it is essentially the return of the West to a traditional civilization, in its principles

---

2. Let us recall here Max Müller's very explicit admission: 'This concentration of thought, *ekāgrata* (or *ekāgrya*) or one-pointedness, as the Hindus called it, is something to us almost unknown. Our minds are like kaleidoscopes of thoughts in constant motion; and to shut our mental eyes to everything else, while dwelling on one thought only, has become to most of us almost as impossible as to appreciate one musical note without harmonics. With the life we are leading now ... it has become impossible, or almost impossible, ever to arrive at that intensity of thought which the Hindus meant by *ekāgrata* and the attainment of which was to them the indispensable condition of all philosophical and religious speculation.' (Preface to the *Sacred Books of the East*, pp xxiii–xxiv.) It would be impossible to give a better description of the scattered nature of the Western outlook, and we have only two corrections to make to this text: what concerns the Hindus should be put into the present as well as the past, since for them it remains always so, and there can be no question here of 'philosophical and religious speculation', but of 'metaphysical speculation' exclusively.

and in the whole mass of its institutions. This return will have to be brought about in the proper order, going from the principles to the consequences, and descending by degrees down to the most contingent applications; and it can only be done by using both what the East has to offer and also whatever traditional elements remain in the West herself, the former completing the latter and being superposed on them—not modifying them in themselves but giving them, by revealing their deepest meaning, their own original point and purpose in all its fullness. As we have said, a firm stand must first of all be taken at the intellectual point of view, and by a perfectly natural repercussion the consequences will then spread in due course, more or less quickly, to all the other domains, including that of social applications. If some useful work should have already been accomplished by other means in these other domains, there will obviously be no cause to be anything but thankful, but it is not to this end that efforts should be directed at first, for that would mean putting the accessory above the essential. Until the right moment comes, the considerations that have to do with secondary points of view ought scarcely to enter in except as examples, or rather as 'illustrations'; as such, if presented relevantly and under a suitable form, they can have the advantage of making the most essential truths more easily understood by supplying a kind of foothold, and also of arousing the attention of people who, through a faulty appreciation of their own faculties, might believe themselves incapable of reaching pure intellectuality without moreover knowing what it is; let everyone remember what we said above about the unexpected means which may on occasion be the deciding factor at the outset of an intellectual development. It is necessary to mark out an absolute distinction between the essential and the accidental; but once this distinction has been made we have no wish to set any restrictive bounds to the part played by the elite, in which each one will always be able to find means of using his own special talents as it were in addition and without any detriment whatsoever to the essential. In short, the elite will work first for itself, since its members will naturally reap from their own development an immediate and altogether unfailing benefit, one moreover that amounts to a permanent and inalienable acquisition; but at the same time, and by that very development, it will necessarily be working, though less immediately, for the West in general as well, since it is impossible that work such as this should be brought to fruit in any surroundings without producing there sooner or later considerable modifications. Besides, mental currents are subject to perfectly definite laws, and the knowledge of these laws makes for action that is incomparably more effective than the use of means simply derived from experience; but here, to succeed in making the application and in giving it its full realization, there must be a strongly constituted organization to rely on, which does not mean to say that partial results, already appreciable, may not be obtained before this point be reached. However defective and incomplete the means at one's disposal may be, the first thing to be done is to bring them into action as they are, for otherwise there will be no possibility of ever acquiring more perfect ones. We will add that the least thing accomplished according to the principles carries virtually in itself possibilities whose expansion may serve to bring about the most tremendous consequences; and this affects not merely one particular realm but all, insofar as the repercussions spread themselves throughout the full hierarchy in indefinite progression.[3]

Naturally, in speaking of the part to be played by the elite, we are supposing that there will be no sharp and sudden event to interrupt its action; in other words, we are considering the most favorable possibility. It is also possible—for there are discontinuities in history—that the Western civilization might be blotted out in some cataclysm before this action had been carried out. If such a thing were to happen before the elite had been fully constituted, the results of the previous work would evidently be limited to the intellectual benefits reaped by those who had taken part in it; but these

3. We allude to an extremely important metaphysical theory which we name 'theory of gesture', and which we will perhaps expound one day in a special treatise. The word 'progression' is taken here in a sense analogous to its mathematical one, but transposed so as to make it applicable in the universal order, no longer confining it to the single domain of quantity. See also, in connection with this, what we have already said elsewhere about *apūrva* and 'concordant actions and reactions': *Introduction to the Study of the Hindu Doctrines*, pt. 3, chap. 13.

benefits are, by themselves, something inestimable, and so, even if there were nothing else forthcoming, this work would still be worthwhile; the fruits would then be withheld from all save a few, but these few, as far as they themselves were concerned, would have got the essential.

If the elite were already constituted, even though it had not time to act generally enough upon the West so as to bring about a deep alteration in her whole mentality, there would be something more: during the period of trouble and upheaval this elite would be the symbolic ark floating on the waters of the flood, and, afterward, it could serve as a point of support for an action by which the West, though probably losing her autonomous existence, would nonetheless receive, from the other remaining civilizations, the principles of a new development, this time regular and normal. But in the second case there would still be, at least for a time, lamentable prospects to consider: the ethnic revolutions that we have already alluded to would certainly be very serious; besides, it would be far better for the West, instead of being absorbed purely and simply, to be able to transform herself so as to acquire a civilization comparable to those of the East, but adapted to her own conditions, and absolving her, as far as the bulk of the people was concerned, from having to assimilate, more or less painfully, traditional forms which were not made for her. This transformation, taking place smoothly and spontaneously, in order to give the West once more an appropriate traditional civilization, is what we have just called the most favorable possibility. Such would be the work of the elite, with the aid no doubt of those who are in charge of the Eastern traditions, but with a Western initiative as starting point; and it should be understood now that this last condition, even if it were not as rigorously indispensable as it actually is, would make nonetheless for a considerable advantage, since this initiative would be the means of the West's preserving her autonomy and even keeping, for her future development, those not worthless elements which she may after all have acquired in her present civilization. In short, if there were time for this possibility to be realized, the catastrophe that we began by considering would be avoided, since the Western civilization, normal once more, would have its legitimate place among the others and would no longer be, as it is today, a menace to the rest of humanity, a factor of disequilibrium, and oppression in the world. In any case, action should be taken as if the said goal must inevitably be reached, because, even if circumstances make it impossible, nothing of what has been achieved toward it will be lost; and to have this goal in view may supply those who are capable of belonging to the elite with a motive for striving to understand pure intellectuality, this motive being by no means negligible while they are still not fully conscious of something less contingent, that is, of what intellectuality is worth in itself, apart from the results that it may produce additionally in the more or less outward orders. The prospect of these results then, however secondary, may be at least a help, and it cannot moreover be an obstacle so long as care is taken to put it exactly in its place and to observe in everything the necessary hierarchies, so as never to lose sight of the essential or sacrifice it to the accidental. We have already given enough explanation on this score to justify, in the eyes of those who understand these things, the standpoint which we adopt here, and which, if it does not correspond to our whole thought (and it could not, seeing that purely doctrinal and speculative considerations rank for us above all others), represents nonetheless a very real part of it.

We make no claim to consider here anything more than possibilities that are in all likelihood very remote, but that are nonetheless possibilities, and that, for this alone, deserve to be taken into account; moreover the very fact of considering them may perhaps be already a step, in some measure, toward bringing their realization closer. Besides, in an essentially restless atmosphere such as that of the modern West, events may take place under the action of certain circumstances, with a speed far surpassing all expectations; it cannot therefore be too soon to set about getting ready to face them, and it is better to look too far ahead than to let oneself be taken unawares by an irremediable calamity. Certainly, we have no illusions as to the chances that such warnings have of being listened to by most of our contemporaries; but, as we have said, the intellectual elite would not need to be very large, especially at the beginning, to enable its influence to have a very effective action, even upon those who had not the slightest idea of its existence or who did not in the very least suspect the range of its work. Here comes to light the uselessness of those 'secrets' that we alluded to earlier: there are actions which, by their very nature, remain totally unknown to the ordinary man, not because they are concealed from him, but because he is incapable of understanding them. There would be no question of the elite making public the means of its action, chiefly because it would be pointless, and because, even if it wanted to, it would not be able to explain them in language that could be understood by the vast majority; it would know in advance that it would be a waste of time, and that the efforts so spent might be put to a better use. We do not contest, moreover, the danger and untimeliness of certain things being divulged: many people might be tempted, if the means were shown them, to set certain forces in motion for the sake of results that they were in no way ready for, simply and solely out of curiosity, without understanding the true point of them, and without knowing where they might lead. This would only be a supplementary cause of disequilibrium, a most deplorable addition to all those that are making for turmoil in the Western mind today and that will no doubt go on doing so for some time yet, and one that would be all the more to be dreaded owing to the deeper nature of the things brought into play: but all who have certain kinds of knowledge are, by virtue of that alone, fully qualified to appreciate such dangers, and they will always know how to behave in consequence without being bound by other obligations than those which are quite naturally implied in the degree of intellectual development that they have reached. Besides, the first step to be taken is necessarily that of theoretic preparation, which is the one essential and truly indispensable preparation, and theory can always be put forward without reserve, or at least with the sole reserve of what is strictly inexpressible and incommunicable. It is for each one to understand insofar as he is capable, and, as for those who do not understand, if they reap no advantage from it, they suffer no harm from it either, remaining simply as they were before. Perhaps some will be surprised that we should lay so much stress on things that are on the whole extremely simple and ought not to raise the least difficulty; but experience has shown us that too many precautions cannot be taken in this respect, and we would rather over-explain certain points than risk seeing our thought wrongly interpreted. The remarks we have still to make are prompted largely by the same anxiety, and as they come in answer to a lack of understanding that we have actually met with face to face on several occasions, they will prove well enough that there is nothing exaggerated in our fear of being misunderstood.

4

NOT FUSION BUT MUTUAL UNDERSTANDING

ALL THE EASTERN CIVILIZATIONS, despite the very great difference of the forms that they are dressed in, may be compared with each other, because they are all essentially traditional in character; each tradition has its own ways of expression, and its own modalities, but, wherever there is tradition, in the true and deep sense of the word, there is necessarily agreement on the principles. The differences lie solely in the outward form, in the contingent applications, which are naturally conditioned by circumstances, above all by racial characteristics, and which, for a given civilization, may even vary within certain limits, since that is the domain which is left open to adaptation. But where there is no longer anything but outward forms, which reflect nothing of any deeper order, there can hardly be any longer anything but differences with regard to the other civilizations. There is no longer any agreement possible as soon as there are no longer any principles, and that is why the lack of actual attachment to a tradition seems to us the very root of the Western deviation. That is also why we declare in so many words that, if the intellectual elite comes one day to be constituted, the essential end which it will have to work for is the return of the West to a traditional civilization; and we will add that if there has ever been a properly Western development in this sense, we have the example of it in the Middle Ages, so that it would be on the whole a question, not of copying or reconstituting purely and simply what existed then (a task that would obviously be impossible, for, whatever certain people may maintain, history does not repeat itself, and there are merely analogous things in the world, not identical things), but of drawing inspiration from it for the adaptation made necessary by the circumstances. That is, word for word, what we have always said, and it is not without express intention that we reproduce it here in the same terms that we have already used;[1] this seems to us clear enough to leave no room for any doubt. However, there are some who have shown the strangest misunderstanding on this score, and who have thought fit to attribute to us the most fantastic intentions, for example that of wanting to restore something comparable to the Alexandrian 'syncretism'. We will come back to that directly, but let us make it quite clear to begin with that when we speak of the Middle Ages, we have particularly in mind the period beginning with Charlemagne's reign and going down to the end of the thirteenth century—which is rather remote from Alexandria! It is indeed curious that when we maintain the fundamental unity of all the traditional doctrines, we can be taken as meaning that the task in question is a 'fusion' between the different traditions, and that people should fail to see that agreement about the principles in no way presupposes uniformity. Does not this seem to be yet another outcome of that very Western fault of not being able to go further than outward appearances? In any case, we do not think it a waste of words to revert to this question and to lay further stress on it, so as to save our intentions from being any longer misrepresented in this way; and, besides, apart from this consideration, the question is not without interest.

In virtue of the principles being universal, as we have said, all the traditional doctrines are identical in essence; there is and can only be one metaphysics, however differently it may be expressed, insofar as it actually is expressible, according to the language at one's disposal, which moreover merely serves as a symbol and never as anything more; and this is so quite simply because the truth is one, and because, being in itself absolutely independent of our conceptions, it imposes itself alike on all those who understand it. Two veritable traditions, then, can never in any instance be in contradiction with each other. If there are doctrines that are incomplete (whether they have always been so or whether part of them has been

---

1. *Introduction to the Study of the Hindu Doctrines.*

lost), and that may be more or less far-reaching, it is nonetheless true that up to the point where they stop they remain in agreement with the others, even though their living representatives should be unaware of it. For all that lies beyond, there can be no question either of agreement or of disagreement; but only the systematic mind could call in question the existence of this 'beyond', and apart from this biased negation, which is a little too like those that are second nature to the modern mind, all that the incomplete doctrine can do is to admit itself incompetent with regard to what goes beyond it. In any case, if two traditions were found to be in apparent contradiction with one another, the right conclusion would be, not that one was true and that the other was false, but that at least one of them was not fully understood; and on a closer examination it would be seen that there was in fact one of those mistakes of interpretation which the differences in expression, for anyone not sufficiently used to them, may very easily give rise to. As for us, more-over, we must say that in point of fact we do not find such contradictions, while on the contrary we see in a very clear light, beneath the most diverse forms, the essential unity of doctrine. What amazes us is that those who assume on principle the existence of one 'primordial tradition', originally common to all mankind, do not see the consequences implied in this affirmation or do not know how to draw them from it, and that they are sometimes just as rabidly anxious as others to discover oppositions which are purely imaginary. We are only speaking, of course, of the doctrines that are truly traditional, or, if it be preferred, 'orthodox'; there are means of recognizing these doctrines among all the others without any possible mistake, just as there are also means of determining the exact degree of understanding that any one doctrine corresponds to; but that does not concern us at the moment. To sum up what we think in a few words, we can say this: every truth is exclusive of error, not of another truth (or, to express ourselves better, of another aspect of the truth); and, we repeat, all exclusivism other than that is nothing more than the mark of a systematic outlook, which is incompatible with the understanding of the universal principles.

Since the agreement is essentially on principles, it can only be truly conscious for those doctrines that have in them at least a part of metaphysics or of pure intellectuality; it is not conscious for those strictly limited to a special form, for example that of religion. However, this agreement exists nonetheless really in such a case, in that the theological truths may be considered as an adaptation of certain metaphysical truths to a special point of view; but to show this, the transposition must be made which gives back to these truths their deepest meaning, and only the metaphysician can make it, because he places himself beyond all the particular forms and all the special points of view. Metaphysics and religion are not, and never will be, on the same plane; it follows, furthermore, that a purely metaphysical doctrine and a religious doctrine cannot enter into rivalry or conflict, since their domains are clearly different. But, on the other hand, it follows also that the existence of a solely religious doctrine is not enough to allow the establishment of a deep mutual understanding like the one we have in view when we speak of intellectual relations being renewed between East and West. That is why we have insisted on the necessity of carrying out in the first place work of a metaphysical order, and it is only then that the religious tradition of the West, revived and restored in its fullness, could come to be of use for this end, thanks to the addition of the inner element which it now lacks, but which might very well succeed in superposing itself without there being any outward change. If a mutual understanding is possible among the representatives of the different traditions—and we know that there is nothing against it in principle—this understanding can only be brought about from above, in such a way that each tradition will always keep its full independence, with the forms that belong to it; and the masses, while sharing in the advantages of this understanding, will not be directly conscious of it, for that is something which only concerns the elite, and even 'the elite of the elite', according to the expression used by certain Islamic schools.

It is obvious how remote all this is from all those schemes of 'fusion' which we consider to be utterly impracticable. A tradition is not a thing that can be invented or artificially created. However well or badly elements borrowed from different traditions be put together, the result will never be more than a pseudo-tradition without value and without bearing, and such fantastic ideas should be left to the occultists and the Theosophists. To act as they do means ignorance of what a tradition truly is and failure to understand the real and deep meaning of these elements that they strive to fit together into a more or less incoherent assemblage. In fact, it is all no more than a sort of 'eclecticism', and there is nothing that we are more resolutely against, precisely because we see the deep agreement beneath the diversity of the forms, and because we see also, at the same time, the reason for these many forms in the variety of the conditions that they must be adapted to. The very great importance of studying the different traditional doctrines lies in the scope that it gives for verifying this agreement and harmony which we affirm here; but there can be no question of making this study the source of a new doctrine: such an idea, far from conforming to the traditional outlook, would be absolutely against it. No doubt, when the elements of a certain order are lacking, as is the case in the modern West for all that is purely metaphysical, they must be looked for elsewhere, wherever they actually exist; but it must not be forgotten that metaphysics is essentially universal, so that it is not the same thing as it would be in the case of elements that have reference to a particular domain. Besides, the Eastern forms of expression would never have to be assimilated by any but the elite, which would then have to set about the task of adaptation; and the knowledge of the doctrines of the East would make it possible, by a judicious use of analogy, to restore the Western tradition itself in its entirety, just as it may make it possible to understand the vanished civilizations; these two cases are altogether comparable, since it must be admitted that, for the most part, the Western tradition is now lost.

Where we have in view a synthesis of a transcendent order as the only possible starting-point for all the further realizations, some people imagine that there can only be question of a more or less confused 'syncretism'; however, those are things that have nothing in common, and there is not even the least connection between them. In the same way, there are some who cannot hear the word 'esoterism' (which we do not abuse, as will be admitted) without thinking immediately of occultism or of other things of the same kind, in which there is not a trace of true esoterism. It is incredible that the most unjustified claims should be so easily admitted by those very people who would have most interest in refuting them.

The only effective means of fighting occultism is to show that there is nothing serious in it, that it is only an altogether modern invention, and that esoterism, in the true sense of the word, is in reality something quite different from it. There are also some who, by another confusion, think that 'esoterism' may be glossed by 'gnosticism'; here the conceptions in question are genuinely older, but for all that the interpretation is neither more exact nor more justified. It is rather hard to know now the precise nature of the somewhat varied doctrines which are classed together under the term 'gnosticism', and among which there would no doubt be many distinctions to make; but, on the whole, they seem to have contained more or less disfigured Eastern ideas, probably misunderstood by the Greeks, and clothed in imaginative forms which are scarcely compatible with pure intellectuality; it would assuredly cost little effort to find things more worthy of interest, less mixed with heteroclite elements, of a much less dubious value, and much more surely significant. This leads us up to a few remarks about the Alexandrian period in general: that the Greeks were then in fairly direct contact with the East, and that their outlook was thus opened to conceptions against which it had until then been shut, seems to us beyond all question; but the result seems unfortunately to have remained much nearer to 'syncretism' than to true synthesis. We have no wish to depreciate unduly such doctrines as those of the Neoplatonic school, which are in any case incomparably superior to all the productions of modern philosophy, but when all is said and done it is better to go back directly to the Eastern source than to take any intermediate steps, and, besides, that has the advantage of being much easier, since the Eastern civilizations still exist, whereas the Greek civilization has not really had any direct successors. The Eastern doctrines, once known, may serve as a means for better understanding the Neoplatonic ones, and even ideas more purely Greek than those, for despite some considerable differences the West was then much closer to the East than it is today; but the inverse would not be possible, and anyone who sought to approach the East through Greece would lay himself open to many mistakes. Besides, the wants of the West can only be supplied by addressing oneself to what actually still exists. There can be no question here of archeology, and the things we have in mind have nothing to do with the pastimes of scholars. If the knowledge of antiquity can play a part, it is only insofar as it will help to understand certain ideas properly, and confirm still further that doctrinal unity which is the meeting ground of all civilizations, with the exception of the modern one alone, which, having neither doctrine nor principles, is outside the normal ways of humanity.

If no attempt at fusion between the different doctrines is admissible, still less can there be any question of substituting one doctrine for another; not only is there no disadvantage in there being many traditional forms, but on the contrary there are very definite advantages in it; even though these forms are, at bottom, fully equivalent, each one of them has its point, if only because it is better fitted than any other to the conditions of some particular setting. The tendency to make everything uniform comes, as we have said, from prejudices instilled by those who preach 'equality'; to seek to apply it here would therefore amount to making a concession to the modern outlook, and this concession, even if involuntary, would be nonetheless real, and could only have most deplorable consequences. Only if the West showed herself definitely powerless to go back to a normal civilization could an alien tradition be imposed upon her; but then there would be no fusion, because there would no longer be left anything that was specifically Western; and there would be no substitution either, for, to reach such an extremity, the West would have to have lost even the last vestiges of the traditional outlook—all except for a small elite without which, unable even to receive this alien tradition, she would sink inevitably into the worst barbarism. But, we repeat, it is not too late to hope that things will not go so far and that the elite will be able to establish itself and carry out its task fully, so that the West may not only be saved from chaos and dissolution, but find once more the principles and means of a development that is natural to her, while being at the same time in harmony with that of the other civilizations.

As for the part to be played by the East in all this, let us, to make things clearer, sum it up once more as precisely as possible; we can also make clear, in this connection, the difference between the period of the elite's constitution and that of its effective action. In the first period it is by the study of the Eastern doctrines, more than by any other means, that those who are destined to belong to this elite will be able to acquire and develop in themselves pure intellectuality, since they cannot possibly find it in the West. It is also only by this study that they will be able to learn what a traditional civilization is in its various elements, for it is only a knowledge as direct as possible that has any value in such a case, and there is no place for mere book-learning, which is of no use by itself for the end that we have in view. For the study of the Eastern doctrines to be what it ought to be, certain individuals will have to serve as intermediaries, in the way that we have explained, between the possessors of these doctrines and the Western elite in formation; that is why, for the latter, we speak only of a knowledge as direct as possible, and not absolutely direct, at least to begin with. But subsequently, with the way prepared by this work of assimilation, nothing need stop the elite itself (since it is from it that the initiative must come) from appealing in a more direct way to the representatives of the Eastern traditions; and the latter would be brought to take an interest in the lot of the West by the very presence of this elite and would not fail to answer this appeal, for the one condition that they insist on is understanding (and this one condition is moreover imposed by the very nature of things). We can state definitely that we have never seen any Easterner keep up his habitual reserve when he finds himself face to face with someone whom he thinks capable of understanding him. It is in the second period that actual and visible help of this kind could be given by the Easterners. We have said why that presupposes an elite already constituted, that is, in fact, a Western organization capable of entering into relations with the Eastern organizations which work in the order of pure intellect, and of receiving from them, for its action, the help that is to be had from forces which have accumulated from time immemorial. In such an event the Easterners will always be, for the people of the West, guides and 'elder brothers'; but the West, without claiming to be on a footing of absolute equality with them, will nonetheless have the right to be considered as an independent power as soon as she possesses such an organization; and the Easterners' deep distaste for anything that smacks of proselytism will be sufficient guarantee of her independence. The Easterners are not in the least bent on absorbing the West, and they will always much prefer to help on a Western development in conformity with the principles, however little possibility they see of this; it is precisely for those who are to belong to the elite to show them this possibility, proving by their own example that the intellectual degradation of the West is not past all cure. The thing to be done, then, is not to impose on the West an Eastern tradition whose forms would not correspond to the people's mentality, but to restore a Western tradition with the help of the East, first with indirect help, then direct, or, in other words, inspiration in the first period and actual support in the second. But what is not possible for Westerners in general will have to be so for the elite: before it can hope to carry out the necessary adaptations, it must first have penetrated and understood the traditional forms that exist elsewhere; it must also go beyond all forms, whatever they may be, to grasp what constitutes the essence of all tradition. It is in virtue of this that, when the West is once more in possession of a regular and traditional civilization, the elite will be bound to play its part still further: it will then be the means by which the Western civilization will communicate permanently with the other civilizations, for such a communication can only be established and kept up by what is highest in each of them. In order that it may not be simply at the mercy of events, there must be men present who are, for their own part, detached from all particular forms, fully conscious of what is behind the forms, and who, placing themselves in the domain of the most transcendent principles, may take part in all the traditions without distinction. In other words, the West would finally have to reach the stage of having representatives in what is symbolically termed the 'center of the world' or its equivalent (which should not be taken literally as indicating any fixed place whatsoever); but this question is concerned with things too remote and, for the moment and no doubt for some time to come, too inaccessible for there to be any advantage in insisting on it.[2]

Since the first step toward rousing Western intellectuality from its slumber must be the study of the doctrines of the East (we mean a real and deep study, with everything that it includes concerning the

2. See *The King of the World*. ED.

personal development of those who undertake it, and not an outward and superficial study after the manner of the orientalists), we must now explain why one of these doctrines is, in general, to be approached rather than the others. It might in fact be asked why we take India as our mainstay rather than China, or why we do not think more is to be gained from basing our work on what is closest to the West, that is, on the esoteric side of the Islamic doctrine. We will confine ourselves, moreover, to considering these three big divisions of the East; all the rest is, either of lesser importance, or, like the Tibetan doctrines, so unknown to the Europeans that it would be very difficult to speak to them intelligibly about them before they had understood things less completely foreign to their usual way of thinking. As for China, there are similar reasons for not fixing on her to begin with; the forms in which her doctrines are expressed are really too far removed from the Western mentality, and the methods of teaching in use there are such as might immediately discourage the most gifted Europeans; very few indeed are those who could bear up under work directed along such lines, and, if the prospect of a very rigorous selection should in any case be kept in mind, one should nonetheless avoid as much as possible difficulties that would merely depend on contingencies, and which would arise rather from the temperament inherent in the race than from a real lack of intellectual faculties. The forms of expression of the Hindu doctrines, while being also extremely unlike all those that Western thought is used to, are to be assimilated with relatively greater ease, and they have in them greater possibilities of adaptation. We might say, taking the East as a whole, that India, being in the middle, is neither too far from the West nor too near her for our present purpose. In fact, there would also be disadvantages in taking what is nearest as a basis, and though these would be of a different kind from the ones that we have just been pointing out, they would nonetheless be quite serious enough; and perhaps there would not be many real advantages to make up for them, as Westerners are almost as ill-informed about the Islamic civilization as they are about the more Eastern ones, and the metaphysical part of it in particular, which is what interests us here, escapes them altogether. It is true that this Islamic civilization, with its two aspects, esoteric and exoteric, and with the religious form which the latter is clothed in, comes nearest to being like what a traditional Western civilization would be; but the very presence of this religious form, by which Islam takes as it were after the West, might arouse certain susceptibilities which, however little justified they were, would not be without danger. Those who are incapable of distinguishing between the different domains would wrongly imagine there to be a rivalry between the religions; and there is certainly, among the Western masses (in which we include most of the pseudo-intellectuals), much more hatred against all that is Islamic than against what concerns the rest of the East. Fear enters a good deal into the motives of this hatred, and this state of mind is only due to lack of understanding, but, so long as it exists, the most elementary forethought demands that it shall not be altogether ignored. The elite on its way to being formed will have quite enough to do in the way of overcoming the hostility which it will run up against on different sides, without pointlessly adding to this hostility by making room for false suppositions which stupidity and malignity combined would not fail to give credit to; there will probably be some in any case, but, when they can be foreseen, it is better to take steps against their materializing, if at least it is possible to do so without incurring other consequences that would be still worse. That is why we do not think it advisable to take as our mainstay Islamic esoterism; but, naturally, that does not mean that this esoterism, being truly metaphysical in its essence, has not the equivalent to offer of what is to be found in the other doctrines; all this, then, we repeat, is merely a question of opportuneness, which only arises because it is as well to select the most favorable conditions for work, and does not involve the principles themselves.

Moreover, if we take the Hindu doctrine as the center of the study in question, that does not mean that we intend to refer to it exclusively; it is important on the contrary to bring out, at every favorable opportunity, the agreement and equivalence of all the metaphysical doctrines. It must be shown that beneath expressions that vary there are conceptions that are identical because they correspond to the same truth; sometimes even there are analogies that strike one all the more because they have bearing on very particular points, and also there is a certain community of symbols among the different traditions. These are things that it would be impossible to overemphasize, and there is no question of 'syncretism' or 'fusion' in establishing these real likenesses and this sort of parallelism which exists among all the civilizations that are traditional, and which can only be surprising to men who believe in no transcendent truth both beyond and above human conceptions. For our part, we do not think that civilizations like those of India and China need necessarily have been in direct communication with one another in the course of their development; that does not prevent them from having, side by side with very marked differences that are to be explained by ethnic and other conditions, features in which they are noticeably alike; and here we are not speaking of the metaphysical order, where the equivalence is always perfect and absolute, but of the applications made to the order of contingent things. Of course, one must always keep in mind the possibility of something belonging to the 'primordial tradition'; but since this is by definition previous to the special development of the civilizations in question, its existence does not take away any of their independence. Besides, the 'primordial tradition' must be considered as having essentially to do with the principles, and in this domain there has always been a certain lasting communication, established from within and from above, as we have just been saying; but that also does not affect the independence of the different civilizations. However, in the face of certain symbols which are the same everywhere, there is clearly nothing for it but to acknowledge them to be a manifestation of this fundamental traditional unity which is so generally unrecognized today, and which the 'scientists' are at great pains to discount as something particularly annoying; the existence of such points in common cannot be mere chance, especially as the ways of expression are, in themselves, apt to vary indefinitely. In short, unity, for whoever has eyes to see it, is everywhere, underlying all diversity; it is there in consequence of the universality of the principles. That the truth should impress itself in the same way on men who have no direct connection with one another, or that real intellectual relations should be kept up between the representatives of different civilizations, is only made possible by this universality;

and, if it were not consciously admitted by one or two at least, there could be no question of any truly stable and deep agreement. What all normal civilizations have in common are the principles; if these were lost sight of, each civilization would have scarcely anything left but the special characteristics by which it differs from the others, and even the likenesses would become purely superficial since the true reason for them would not be known. We do not mean that it is absolutely wrong to cite, in explanation of certain general likenesses, the unity of human nature; but it is usually done in a very vague and altogether inadequate way, and moreover the mental differences are much greater and go much further than those who only know one type of humanity can imagine. This unity itself cannot be clearly understood and given its full significance without a true knowledge of the principles, apart from which it is somewhat illusory; the true nature of the species and its deep reality are things that no mere empiricism could account for.

But let us revert to what led us up to these considerations: there cannot be the slightest question of 'specializing' in the study of the Hindu doctrine, since the order of pure intellect is just what eludes all specialization. All the doctrines that are metaphysically complete are fully equivalent, and we can even say that they are necessarily identical at bottom; it only remains, then, to decide which is the one that would lend itself most to the sort of exposition required, and we think that, in a general way, it is the Hindu doctrine; that is the reason, and that alone, why we take it as a basis. But if it should happen that certain points are treated of by other doctrines under a form that seems easier to assimilate, there can clearly be no harm in having recourse to those doctrines; in fact it would be yet another way of bringing to light that agreement which we have just been speaking of. We will go further: tradition, instead of standing in the way of the adaptations called for by circumstances, has on the contrary always provided the principle which all necessary adaptations could be based on, and these are absolutely legitimate through their keeping to the strictly traditional line, or, in other words, to what we have also termed 'orthodoxy'. So, if new adaptations are called for, as is all the more natural on account of the difference in the setting, there is no harm in formulating them by drawing inspiration from those that exist already, while taking also the mental conditions of this setting into account, provided that it is done with the required forethought and competence, and that the traditional outlook has already been grasped in all its depth with all that it includes; this is what the intellectual elite will have to do sooner or later, in everything for which no earlier Western form of expression can be found. It is clear how remote this is from the standpoint of scholarship: the origin of a particular idea does not interest us in itself, for this idea, in being true, is independent of all the men who have expressed it under this form or that; historical contingencies are irrelevant. But since we do not claim to have reached by ourselves and without any help the ideas which we know to be true, we think that it will be as well for us to say who passed them on to us, especially since by so doing we shall be pointing out to others which way they can turn so as to find them for themselves; and, in fact, it is to the Easterners alone that we owe these ideas. As to the question of age, if only considered in a historical way, it is not of very great interest either; only when connected with the idea of tradition does it take on quite another aspect, but then, if it be understood what tradition really is, this question loses its point at once through the knowledge that from the beginning everything was implied principially in what is the very essence of the doctrines, so that it merely had to be deduced from the principles later by a development which, in its foundation if not in its form, could not admit of any innovation. There is no doubt that a certainty of this kind is scarcely communicable; but, if some people possess it, why should not others attain to it as well, especially if the means are given them insofar as they can be given? The 'chain of the tradition' is sometimes renewed in a very unexpected way; and men have thought that they had conceived certain ideas spontaneously whereas they had in fact received help that was effective in spite of not being consciously felt by them; still less should such help fail those who put themselves expressly in the required disposition for obtaining it. Of course, we are not denying here the possibility of direct intellectual intuition, since we maintain on the contrary that it is absolutely indispensable and that without it there is no real metaphysical conception; but it must be led up to, and whatever latent faculties an individual may have, we doubt if he can develop them by himself; at the very least a certain event is necessary to make way for this development. This event, which may vary indefinitely according to the particular cases is never accidental except in appearance; in reality, it is brought about by an action whose ways of working, although they inevitably escape all outside observation, may be grasped by those who understand that 'spiritual posterity' is no empty phrase. However, it should be said that cases of this sort are always exceptional, and that if they occur in the absence of all unbroken and regular transmission carried out by organized traditional teaching (one or two examples of such cases might be found in Europe, as also in Japan), they can never entirely make up for this absence, firstly because they are few and far between, and secondly because they lead to the acquisition of knowledge which, whatever its value, is never more than fragmentary. It should also be added that the means of coordinating and expressing what is conceived in this way cannot be given at the same time, so that the benefit remains almost exclusively a personal one.[3] True, that is already something, but it must not be forgotten that even from the point of view of this personal profit, a partial and incomplete realization, like that which may be had in such a case, is a poor result compared with the veritable metaphysical realization that all the Eastern doctrines assign to man as his supreme goal (and which, let us say in passing, has absolutely nothing to do with 'quietist sleep' as is imagined by some people that we have come across, through a grotesque interpretation that is certainly not justified by anything we have said of it). Besides, where realization has not been preceded by a sufficient theoretic preparation, many confusions may arise, and there is always the possibility of losing one's way in one of those intermediate domains where there is no security against illusions; it is only in the domain of pure metaphysics that such security is to be had, and, since it is then acquired once and for all, there can no longer be the least danger in entering any other domain whatsoever, as we have already pointed out.

3. The connection might be noted between this and what we have said elsewhere with regard to 'mystical states'; the two states are, if not identical, at least comparable; we shall no doubt have to revert to this question on other occasions.

The truth of facts may seem almost negligible compared with the truth of ideas; however, even in the contingent order, there are degrees to be observed, and there is a way of looking at things, by linking them up with their principles, which gives them an importance such as they altogether lack by themselves; what we have said about the 'traditional sciences' should be enough to make this clear. There is no need to become involved in questions of chronology, which are often insoluble, at least by the ordinary historical methods; but there is some point in knowing that such and such ideas belong to a traditional doctrine, and even that such and such a way of presenting them is equally traditional in character; we think it unnecessary to insist on this any more, after all the considerations that we have already put forward. In any case, although the truth of facts, which is merely supplementary, must not make one lose sight of the truth of ideas, which is the essential, it would be wrong to refuse to take into account the additional advantages to be had from knowing a fact, since, despite their being, like it, contingent, they are not always to be disdained. To know that certain ideas have been given us by the Easterners is to know a true fact; this is less important than to understand these ideas and to acknowledge inwardly that they are true, and if they had come to us from elsewhere, we would see not the slightest reason for waving them aside *a priori*; but since we have found nowhere in the West the equivalent of these Eastern ideas, we think it as well to say so. Of course, it would be possible to have an easy success by putting forward certain conceptions as if one had, as it were, invented them from start to finish, and by keeping their real origin secret; but we cannot admit such behavior, and besides, it would amount in our eyes to robbing the conceptions of their true bearing and their authority, since in this way they would be reduced to seeming no more than a 'philosophy', when really they are something quite different; here once more we are touching on the question of the individual and the universal, which is at the bottom of all such distinctions.

But let us keep, for the moment, to what is contingent: to maintain boldly that it is in the East that pure intellectual knowledge may be acquired, while striving at the same time to reawaken the intellectuality of the West, is to help promote, in the only effective way, the renewal of relations between East and West; and we hope that it will now be understood why this possibility is not to be neglected, since that is the chief object of all that we have said so far. The restoration of a normal civilization in the West may be only a contingency; but, we repeat, is that a reason for losing all interest in it, even if one is above all a metaphysician? And besides, apart from the importance that such things have in their own relative order, they may be the means of realizations that are not limited to the domain of contingency, and that, for all those who take part in them directly or even indirectly, will have consequences before which all transitory things efface themselves and vanish. The reasons for all this are many, and the deepest of them are perhaps not those that we have laid most stress on, since we could not think of expounding here the metaphysical theories (and even cosmological ones in certain cases, as, for example, where the 'cyclic laws' are concerned) without which they could not be fully understood; we intend to do so in other works which will follow in due course. As we said at the beginning, we cannot possibly explain everything at once; but we state nothing gratuitously, and we are conscious of having, for want of many other merits, at least that of only talking about what we know. If then there are some who are surprised at certain considerations that they are not used to, we hope that they will take the trouble to give them their more attentive reflection, and perhaps they will then see that these considerations, far from being useless or superfluous, are precisely some of the most important, or that what seemed to them at first sight to take us away from our subject is on the contrary what concerns it most directly. There are indeed things that are connected in a way quite different from what is usually thought, and the truth has many aspects that most Westerners scarcely suspect; that is why we should always be more afraid of seeming to limit things too much by the expression that we give them than of implying possibilities that are too great.

CONCLUSION

AFTER WHAT HAS ALREADY BEEN SAID, we might almost do without a conclusion that seems fairly obvious and that would scarcely give us scope for anything more than a repetition, in a more or less summary form, of one or two considerations which we have already treated at length with enough stress to bring out all their importance. We think in fact that we have shown as clearly and explicitly as possible what are the chief prejudices that keep the West of today so remote from the East; and if they do so, it is because they are opposed to true intellectuality, which the East has kept in its fullness, while the West has gone so far as to lose all notion of it, having no longer even the vaguest and most muddled glimmering of it. Those who have understood this will have inevitably grasped as well how 'accidental', in all the various senses of this word, is the divergence that separates the West from the East; the bringing of these two portions of mankind together and the return of the West to a normal civilization are really just one and the same thing, and that is indeed the chief point of their being brought together, as perhaps in the more or less remote future they may be according to the considerations we have put forward. What we call a normal civilization is one that is based on principles, in the true sense of this word, one where everything is arranged in hierarchy to conform to these principles, so that everything in it is seen as the application and extension of a doctrine whose essence is purely intellectual and metaphysical: this is what we mean also when we speak of a traditional civilization. It must not be believed, moreover, that tradition can cramp thought in the slightest, unless it be maintained that to stop it from going astray amounts to limiting it, which we cannot admit; is it permissible to say that the shutting out of error is a limitation of the truth? To reject impossibilities, which are a mere nothing, is not to place restrictions on the total and universal possibility, which is necessarily infinite; it follows that error is a mere negation, a 'privation' in the Aristotelian sense of the word; it has, insofar as it is error (for it may contain fragments of truth that have not been understood), nothing positive, and that is why it may be excluded without laying oneself in the least open to the charge of having a systematic mind. Tradition, on the other hand, admits all the aspects of the truth; it does not set itself against any legitimate adaptation; it allows those who understand it conceptions not only of an immensity that none of the dreams of the most 'daring' philosophers can approach, but also conceptions of a most undreamlike solidity and validity; in short, it opens up possibilities to the intelligence, which, like truth itself, are unlimited.

All this results immediately from the characteristics of metaphysical knowledge, which is indeed the only altogether unlimited knowledge, being of the universal order; and we think it would be as well to revert here to the question, which we have already treated elsewhere, of the relations between metaphysics and logic.[1] Logic, which refers to the conditions that specially belong to human understanding, is something contingent; it is of the individual and rational order, and what are called its principles are only principles in a relative sense; we mean that they can only be, like those of mathematics or of any other particular science, the application and specification, in a fixed domain, of the veritable principles. Thus metaphysics necessarily dominates logic as it dominates all the rest; not to recognize this is to turn upside down the hierarchic relations that are inherent in the nature of things; but, however evident this may appear to us, we have been unable to help noticing that most of our contemporaries find cause for astonishment at it. They are totally ignorant about what is of the metaphysical and 'supra-individual' order; they only know things that belong to the rational order, including the 'pseudo-metaphysics' of the modern philosophers and, in this rational order, logic does actually hold the highest rank, all the rest being subordinate to it. But true metaphysics cannot be dependent on logic any more than on any other science whatsoever; the mistake of those who think that it can comes from their failure to conceive of knowledge apart from the domain of

---

1. *Introduction to the Study of the Hindu Doctrines.*

reason, and from their not having the least suspicion of what pure intellectual knowledge is. This we have already said; and we have also taken care to point out that there is a distinction to be made between the conception of metaphysical truths, which, in itself, is beyond the reach of all individual limitation, and the formulated exposition of them, which, insofar as it is possible, can only be a sort of transposition down to the plane of discourse and reason. If, then, this exposition takes the form of reasoning, and appears logical and even dialectic, it is because, given the way in which human language is constituted, it would be impossible to say anything without such a form; but that is only an outward thing, which does not in the least affect the truths in question, since they are essentially higher than reason. On the other hand, there are two very different ways of considering logic: there is the Western way, which consists in treating it philosophically, and in striving to tie it down to some systematic conception; and there is the Eastern way, that is, logic constituted as a 'traditional science' and bound up with the metaphysical principles, which moreover give it, like every other science, an incomparably greater bearing. It may be, of course, that the results seem practically the same in many cases, but the difference between the two points of view remains quite undiminished; it is no more possible to contest this than it would be to conclude, owing to outward likenesses between the actions of various individuals, that they were carried out with the same intentions. And here is what we have been leading up to: logic is not, in itself, anything especially 'philosophical', since it exists also where there is none of that very particular mode of thought which may be termed philosophy; if metaphysical truths can, up to a certain point—and always excepting what is inexpressible in them—be clothed in logical form, it is traditional logic, and not philosophical logic, that may serve this purpose; and how could it be otherwise, when philosophy has reached the point of being unable to subsist if it does not deny true metaphysics?

It should be seen from this explanation how we regard logic: if we use a certain dialectic, without which it would be impossible for us to speak of anything at all, it cannot be brought up against us as a contradiction, since there is certainly no philosophizing in it so far as we are concerned. Moreover, even when we are especially engaged in refuting the conceptions of the philosophers, one may be sure that we always know how to keep the distances required by the difference in the points of view: we do not place ourselves on the same footing, as do those who criticize or fight one philosophy in the name of another philosophy; we say what we say because the traditional doctrines have enabled us to understand the absurdity or inanity of certain theories, and, whatever the imperfections that we inevitably bring with us to the task (and that should only be imputed to ourselves), the character of these doctrines is such that it forbids us all compromise. What we have in common with the philosophers can only be dialectic; but that is nothing more, as we use it, than an instrument at the service of principles which they have no knowledge of, so that even this likeness is quite outward and superficial, as is the one that may sometimes be noted between the results of modern science and those of the traditional sciences. Also, we cannot be said to be borrowing the methods of the philosophers, for these methods, as far as they are valid, are not their own, but represent simply something that is the common possession of all men, even of those men who are most far removed from the philosophical point of view; philosophical logic is merely a dwindling of traditional logic, and the latter has precedence over the former. If we insist here on this distinction which seems to us essential, it is not for our personal satisfaction, but because it is important to maintain the transcendent character of pure metaphysics, and because all that proceeds from it, even secondarily and in a contingent order, partakes of this character in a sense, thereby becoming something quite different from the merely profane knowledge of the Western world. What characterizes one kind of knowledge and sets it apart from the others is not only its object, but also the way this object is looked at; and that is why some questions which, by their nature, might have a certain metaphysical bearing, lose it altogether when they are incorporated into a philosophical system. But the distinction between metaphysics and philosophy, which is nonetheless fundamental, and which should never be forgotten by anyone who wishes to understand something about the doctrines of the East (since without it there can be no escape from the danger of false assimilations), is so unfamiliar to Westerners that most of them never succeed in grasping it: thus it is that we were surprised to see it stated here and there that we had spoken of 'Hindu philosophy', when we had precisely set ourselves to show that what exists in India is quite different from philosophy! Perhaps what we have just said about logic will suffer the same fate, and we should be no more surprised than before to be credited, in certain circles, with 'philosophizing' against philosophy, whereas what we are really doing is nonetheless something quite different. If we were expounding, for instance, a mathematical theory, and if someone cared to call it 'physics', we should certainly have no means of stopping him, but all those who understand the meaning of words would know just what to think of it; although the notions in question here are less current, the mistakes that we are trying to prevent can quite well be compared with the above example. If some people are tempted to express certain criticisms based on similar confusions, we warn them that these criticisms would fall wide of their mark, and if we can thus spare them some errors we shall be very glad; but we can do no more, for it is not in our power, nor in anyone's, to give understanding to those who have not the means of it in themselves. If then these ill-founded criticisms are nonetheless forthcoming, we have the right to take no account of them at all: but on the contrary, if we see that we have not yet drawn certain distinctions clearly enough, we will revert to them until the uncertainty be no longer possible, or at least until it can no longer be attributed to anything but incurable blindness or evident bad faith.

The same applies to the means by which the West could approach the East by returning to true intellectuality: we believe that the reflections we have put forward here may dispel many confusions about this as also about our view of the eventual state of the Western world, in case the possibilities that we have in mind should come one day to be realized. However, we obviously cannot claim to foresee all possible misunderstandings; if any really important ones come to light, we shall always do our utmost to dispel them also, and we shall do so all the more gladly because it may give us an excellent opportunity of expressing our thoughts more precisely on certain points. In any case, we shall never let ourselves be turned aside from the course that is mapped out for us by all that we have understood thanks to the traditional doctrines of the East. We address ourselves to those who are able and willing to understand in their turn, wherever they may be and wherever they may come from, but not to those who are liable to be stopped by the most insignificant or illusory obstacle, who have a rooted fear of certain things or of certain words, or who would believe themselves lost if they happened to overstep certain conventional and arbitrary limitations. We do not see, in point of fact, what advantage the intellectual elite could draw from the collaboration of these timorous and fretful creatures; he that is not capable of looking every truth in the face, he that does not feel the force of penetrating into the 'great solitude', according to the expression sanctioned by the Far-Eastern tradition (and which has its equivalent in India), could not go very far in the metaphysical work that we have spoken of, and that all the rest strictly depends on. There seems to be, among certain people, a sort of preconceived determination not to understand; but we do not believe that those whose intellectual possibilities are truly far-reaching will be subject to these idle terrors, for they are well enough balanced to have, almost instinctively, the assurance that they will never run the risk of giving way to any mental dizziness. It is true that this assurance is not fully justified so long as they have not attained to a certain degree of actual development, but the mere fact of possessing it, without even being very clearly aware of it, gives them already a considerable advantage. We are not referring here to those who have a more or less excessive confidence in themselves; those we are speaking of, even if they are not yet aware of it, really put their trust in something much higher than their individuality, since they have a kind of presentiment of these higher states which are to be totally and definitely won by pure metaphysical knowledge. As to the others, who dare go neither too high nor too low, the fact is that they cannot see further than certain barriers, beyond which they can no longer even distinguish the higher from the lower, the true from the false, the possible from the impossible; imagining that the truth must be of the same dimensions as themselves and that it is tied down to an average level, they are at their ease in the 'pigeon-holes' of the philosophic outlook, and, even when they have assimilated certain partial truths, they can never use them to enlarge indefinitely their own understanding. Whether it be due to their own nature, or only to the education that they have received, the limitation of their 'intellectual horizon' has become incurable, so that their bias, if that is their trouble, is truly involuntary, even if they are not altogether unaware of it. Among such people, some are certainly the victims of environment, and their case is indeed the most regrettable; their faculties, which might have had the opportunity of being developed in a normal civilization, have on the contrary been atrophied and repressed to the point of annihilation; and, modern education being what it is, one comes to the conclusion that those who know nothing are the ones who are more likely to have kept intact their intellectual possibilities. Compared with the mental deformations that are the ordinary effect of false learning, ignorance pure and simple really seems to us a lesser evil; and although we put knowledge above everything, this is by no means a paradox on our part nor a piece of inconsequence, for the only knowledge truly worthy of the name in our eyes is utterly different from that which is cultivated by the modern Westerners. And let no one reproach us, on this point or on any others, for having an attitude that is too uncompromising; this attitude is forced on us by the purity of the doctrine, by what we have called 'orthodoxy' in the intellectual sense; and, being moreover exempt from all prejudice, it can never lead us into injustice with regard to anything at all. We admit the whole truth, whatever aspect it shows itself under; but, being neither a skeptic nor an eclectic, we cannot admit anything apart from the truth.

We are well aware that our point of view is not one that is usually taken up in the West, and that, in consequence, it may be rather difficult to understand all at once; but it goes without saying that we ask no one to adopt it without examination. Our object is merely to urge to reflection those who are still capable of it; each of them will understand what he can, and, however little this may be, it will always be something; besides, we are very inclined to think that there will be some who will go further. There are no reasons, when all is said and done, why what we have done ourselves should not be done by others also; with the Western mentality as it is, these others will doubtless be no more than exceptions, but it only needs such exceptions to be found, even a few, to justify what we have foreseen and to give the possibilities that we are pointing out a chance of being realized sooner or later. Besides, all that we shall do or say will amount to giving those who come afterward advantages that we ourselves were not given; here, as everywhere else, it is the beginning of the work that is the most painful, and the more unfavorable the conditions, the greater must be the effort toward achievement. The fact that belief in 'civilization' should be more or less shaken in people who until lately would not have dared to dispute it, and that 'scientism' should be undergoing a decline in certain circles, may possibly help us a little, since there is, in consequence, a kind of uncertainty that lets minds embark upon different channels without so much resistance; but that is all we can say about it, and the new tendencies that we have so far noticed are in no way more encouraging than those that they are trying to supplant. From our point of view there is not the slightest difference in value between rationalism and intuitionism, positivism and pragmatism, materialism and spiritualism, 'scientism' and 'moralism'; nothing is gained in passing from one to the other, and no one who is not completely detached from all of them can be said to have taken even the first step in the domain of true intellectuality. We are bent on stating this expressly, just as we are on repeating once again that no study of the Eastern doctrines undertaken 'from the outside' will help in the least toward the end we have in view; what actually will help has quite a different bearing and belongs to a far deeper order of things.

Finally, we will call to the notice of those who eventually gainsay us that if we are fully at our ease in judging quite independently the sciences and philosophies of the West, it is because we are conscious of owing nothing to them; what we are intellectually we owe to the East alone, so that we have behind us nothing that might cramp us in the least. If we have studied philosophy, we did so at a time when our ideas had been completely and definitely fixed on all that is essential, which is probably the only means of not incurring any bad influence from this study; and what we saw then merely confirmed very exactly all that we had been used to thinking with regard to philosophy. We knew that there was no intellectual benefit to be expected from it; and in fact the only help that we did get from it was to be made more aware of the precautions necessary for avoiding confusions, and of the inconveniences that arise from the use of certain terms that are liable to produce uncertainties. These are things that the Easterners are sometimes not enough on their guard against, and there are, in this order, many difficulties of expression which we should not have suspected without having had occasion to examine closely the special language of modern philosophy, with all its incoherences and all its useless subtleties. But this help is merely of service in the work of exposition, because it allows us to anticipate many mistakes of interpretation that are too easily made by those who are used to Western thought and to none other, although at the same time we are forced to introduce complications that have nothing essential in them; for us personally there is not the least advantage in it, since we get no real knowledge from it. If we say this, it is not in order to cite ourselves as an example, but to bring evidence which those who do not in any way share our way of thinking must at least admit as sincere; and if we insist more particularly on our absolute independence with regard to all that is Western, it is because that may help also toward a better understanding of our real intentions. We hold that we have the right to denounce error wherever it is, if we think it timely to do so; but there are disputes that we will not be mixed up in at any price, and we feel that it is not for us to take the side of this or that Western conception; as for what may happen to be of interest in some of these conceptions, we are quite ready to admit it with full impartiality, but we have never found anything in them of any value except a very small fragment of what we already knew from other sources, and wherever the same things were looked at in different ways, it was always the Western points of view that suffered by comparison. It is only after long reflection that we decided to write such a book as this, and we have said why we thought it necessary to do so before dwelling on the doctrine itself, the interest of which may then be brought home to people who for want of preparation would otherwise not have paid enough attention to it, and who nonetheless may be perfectly capable of understanding it.

In being brought nearer to the East, the West has everything to gain; if the East has also some interest in this, it is not an interest of the same order, nor even of an importance that is comparable, and it would not be enough to justify the least concession with regard to what is essential; besides, nothing can be set above the rights which belong to truth. To show the West its faults, its errors, and its shortcomings, is not to evince hostility toward it, but quite the contrary, since it is the only means of curing the evil that it suffers from, and that it may perish of if it does not pull itself together in time. The task is an arduous one certainly, and not without unpleasantness; but that matters little to anyone convinced that it is necessary; we ask no more than that one or two should understand that it is really so. Moreover, no one who has understood this can remain at a standstill, just as no one who has assimilated certain truths can lose sight of them or refuse to accept all the consequences of them; there are obligations which are inherent in all true knowledge, and compared with them all outward ties seem vain and laughable; these obligations, for the very reason that they are purely inward, are the only ones that can never be shaken off. No one can yield to discouragement who has the power of truth on his side, even if he has no other weapon for overcoming the most dreadful obstacles, for this power is such that in the end nothing can prevail against it. The only ones to doubt this are those who do not know that all the partial and transitory disequilibriums go necessarily to make up the great total equilibrium of the Universe.

ADDENDUM

It must be clear to everyone that since this book was written [1924], the situation has grown worse than ever, not merely in the West but in the whole world; this was only to be expected, failing some restoration of order of the kind that we have mentioned, and it goes without saying moreover that we never thought that such a restoration could possibly take place as soon as this. But as a matter of fact the disorder has gone on increasing even more quickly than could have been foreseen, and this should be taken into account, although on the whole it makes no difference to the conclusions which we drew.

In the West the disorder in every sphere has grown so obvious that more and more people are aware of it and begin to doubt the value of modern 'civilization'; but though this is in one sense a favorable sign, the result has so far been purely negative: some people make excellent criticisms of the present state of affairs, but they do not know what remedies to apply, and nothing that they suggest goes beyond the realm of mere contingency, so that it will all be clearly quite ineffective. We can only repeat that the one true remedy lies in the restoration of pure intellectuality; but unfortunately, from this point of view, the chances of a reaction on the part of the West herself seem to grow smaller and smaller, since what is left of tradition in the West is becoming more and more affected by the modern outlook and consequently all the less capable of serving as a sound basis for this restoration, so that without setting altogether aside any possibility that may still exist, it seems likelier than it did before that the East will have to intervene more or less directly, in the way that we explained, if the restoration is eventually to take place.

On the other hand, as far as the East is concerned, it must be admitted that the ravages of 'modernization' have considerably spread, at least outwardly; in those countries that resisted them longest the change seems now to be all the quicker, and India herself is a striking example of this. However, none of it really goes to the heart of the tradition, which is what counts from our point of view, and perhaps it would be wrong to lay too much stress on appearances that may only be transitory; in any case it is enough that the traditional outlook, with all that it implies, should be wholly preserved in some Eastern retreats that are inaccessible to the outward agitation of our age. Besides, it must be remembered that everything modern, even in the East, is really nothing more than a sign that the Western outlook has trespassed there; the real East, the only one that really deserves the name, is and always will be the traditional East, even though its representatives should be reduced to being no more than a minority, as even today is far from the case; it is this East only that we mean, just as, in speaking of the West, we mean the Western outlook, that is, the modern or anti-traditional outlook, wherever it is to be found, since we are above all concerned with the opposition of these two outlooks, and not simply the opposition of two geographical terms. Also, in addition to this, let us say here and now that we are more than ever inclined to think of the traditional outlook, insofar as it is really alive, as remaining intact only in its Eastern forms; however, if the West has still in itself the means of going back to and fully restoring its own tradition, it is for the West to prove it; we can only say that so far we have seen not the slightest sign which would justify us in supposing that it is really capable of carrying out such a task all by itself, even if it should become overwhelmed by the sense of its necessity.

INDEX

agnosticism 31, 39
Alexandria(n) 140, 144
America(ns) 13, 22, 68, 74
Anglo-Saxon 21, 63
apūrva 134 n 3
Arabs 118
Aristotle 53, 127 n 1, 157
Avalokiteshvara 116 n 5

Bacon, Francis 11, 17, 19
Bainville, Jacques 13, 20
Bergson 12, 20, 22, 29, 55, 57–58
Berkeley 15 n 4
Bolshevism 77–79
Bouvet, Rev. Fr. 45–46
Buddhism 99

Cartesian 12, 20, 22, 29
caste(s) 78, 92, 106, 120 n 7
Catholicism 63, 94, 118
Chaldeans 17
Charlemagne 118, 140
China 44–45, 72 n 2, 74, 76, 78, 106, 118, 148, 150
Christendom 118
Comte, Auguste 19, 31, 35, 50
Condorcet 18
Confucianism 47
Couturat 44
Crusades 118

deliverance 59
Descartes 11, 29, 36
Deussen 48, 99

Egyptians 17
ekāgrata (ekāgrya) 132
empericism 64, 151
England 29, 63, 73, 78–79, 96
equality 6, 40, 43, 81, 106, 146
esoterism 117, 143–144, 149
evolution(ism) 18–19, 36, 57, 62

Fu Hsi (Fohy) 44–46, 48, 97
Foucart, Georges 19
Fourier 14
French 63, 77
French Revolution 14

Germany 63, 73, 77, 79, 98–100
gnosticism 144
Greco-Roman 18, 97
Greek(s) 18, 55, 59, 61, 98, 144
Guimet 48 n 9

Hartmann 99
Hindu(s) 30, 48, 59, 78, 91, 94, 99–101, 106, 109, 132 n 2, 148–149, 151, 160
Holbach 15 n 4

I Ching 44, 47–48
India 76, 78, 92, 99, 148, 150, 161
Indo-Germans 100
intuitionism 12, 29, 34, 55, 163
Islam(ic) 76–77, 116, 142, 148–149

James, William 56, 63
Japan(ese) 47, 73–75, 153

Jewish 78
Judaism 78

Kant 32, 51, 61
Keyserling, Count 100 n2
Korea 74
K'ua 45 n6

La Mettrie 15 n4
League of Nations 88
Leibnitz 44–48, 89, 97, 117 n6
Liberal Protestantism 62
Lull, Raymond 44
Lutheran 73

materialism 15, 21–22, 52, 65, 163
moralism 22, 49–50, 60–63, 68, 93, 163
Müller, Max 99, 132 n2
Muslims 78, 93

Neoplatonic 144
Neo-Spiritualism 62, 102
Nominalism 64

Oldenberg 99

Pan-Islamism 76–77
Pascal 17–19
Peking 45, 73
Philastre 48 n10
Poincaré, Henri 39
positivism 163
pragmatism 12, 21, 29, 39, 58, 163
Protestant(ism) 62–63
Pythagorean 48

rationalism 12, 28–29, 32, 34, 50, 54–55, 58, 62, 90, 163
Reformation 62, 118
relativism 31
Renaissance 11, 18, 68
Romans 18, 98
Rousseau 29
Russia(n)(s) 77–79

Saint-Simon 19
Scholastics 117, 127
Schopenhauer 49, 98–99
scientism 35, 60, 63–64, 89, 163
Shankarāchārya 48
Shintoism 73
Spencer 31
Spiritualism 22

Taoism 73
theory of gesture 134 n3
Theosophical movement 100 n2
Theosophist(s) 22, 100–102, 142
Tibetan 116, 148
transformism 57
Trithemius 44
Turgot 18

Upanishads 99

Voltaire 18

Wen-Wang 45 n7
William II 72

yang 48
yellow peril 72–73, 76
yin 48

Printed in the United States
72609LV00003B/149